RE-DISCOVERING
The Twentieth Century World

History revision :
first word war

Titles in this series:

THE SCHOOLS HISTORY PROJECT · OFFICIAL TEXT · S·H·P

RE-DISCOVERING

The Twentieth Century World

A WORLD STUDY AFTER 1900

Colin Shephard
Keith Shephard

Series Editor:
Colin Shephard

Consultant Editor:
Terry Fiehn

Hodder Murray

A MEMBER OF THE HODDER HEADLINE GROUP

The Schools History Project

The Project was set up in 1972, with the aim of improving the study of history for students aged 13–16. This involved a reconsideration of the ways in which history contributes to the educational needs of young people. The Project devised new objectives, new criteria for planning and developing courses, and the materials to support them. New examinations, requiring new methods of assessment, also had to be developed. These have continued to be popular. The advent of GCSE in 1987 led to the expansion of Project approaches into other syllabuses.

The Schools History Project has been based at Trinity and All Saints College, Leeds, since 1978, from where it supports teachers through a biennial Bulletin, regular INSET, an annual conference and a website (www.tasc.ac.uk/shp).

Since the National Curriculum was drawn up in 1991, the Project has continued to expand its publications, bringing its ideas to courses for Key Stage 3 as well as a range of GCSE and A level specifications.

Words printed in SMALL CAPITALS are defined in the Glossary on page 126.

With thanks to Hugh Greany for his work on pages 122–124.

© Colin Shephard, Keith Shephard 1993 with revisions by Terry Fiehn and Keith Shephard 2001

First published in 1993 as part of *Peace and War* by
Hodder Murray (Publishers) Ltd,
338 Euston Road,
London NW1 3BH

This completely revised edition first published 2001

Reprinted 2002 (twice), 2004 (twice), 2005

Layouts by Liz Rowe
Artwork by Art Construction, Jon Davis/Linden Artists, Patricia Ludlow/Linden Artists, Tony Randell, Steve Smith
Colour separations by Colourscript, Mildenhall, Suffolk
Typeset in 11½/13pt Concorde by Wearset, Boldon, Tyne and Wear
Printed and bound in Dubai

A catalogue entry for this title is available from the British Library

ISBN-10: 0 7195 8548 1
ISBN-13: 978 0 7195 8548 7
Teachers' Resource Book ISBN 0 7195 8549 X

Contents

Introduction

1914–18

1933

| 1900 | 1910 | 1920 | 1930 | 1940 |

1940

▼ **ACTIVITY**

1 Match these captions to the photos on the timeline.

■ The Holocaust
■ When the world came closest to nuclear war
■ Germany got a new leader
■ The impact of the first nuclear bomb
■ The Berlin Wall: the beginning of the end of Communism
■ The brave few who saved Britain from a German invasion
■ Off to the trenches

▼ **DISCUSS**

2 a) Which of these events are you most interested in finding out about? Why?
   b) Which of these events do you already know about? What do you know?

1942–45

1962

1950   1960   1970   1980   1990   2000

1945

1989

Your pathway

In this book you will be investigating some of the major events of the twentieth century.

Section 1: The First World War

It was called 'the war to end all wars!' – it was anything but. Four years of trench warfare left millions dead and nothing resolved. You will investigate:

■ how an assassin's bullet in Bosnia triggered the bloodiest war the world had ever known

■ what it was like for ordinary soldiers to take part in the war.

Section 2: The rise of the dictators and the causes of the Second World War

The First World War did not solve Europe's problems – it simply put them on hold. Only a few years later, Germany was in the grip of a dictator, Adolf Hitler, and Europe was once again rushing headlong towards war. In this section you will explore why dictators rose to power and:

Ein Volk, ein Reich, ein Führer!

■ whether or not Hitler should be blamed for starting the Second World War.

Section 3: The Second World War

The Second World War was different from wars that had gone before it. Death and destruction reached new extremes. In this section you will examine key events in the war. You will also focus on:

■ the Home Front – the impact of the war on ordinary people living in Britain

■ the Holocaust – Hitler's attempt to murder Jews and other minority groups

■ the reasons why the first atomic bomb was dropped in 1945 and how it changed the world.

Section 4: The Cold War

In this section you will find out why relations between the USA and the Soviet Union broke down, and why the resulting Cold War was a threat to world peace. In particular, you will consider:

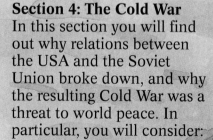

■ the Cuban Missile Crisis and how close the world came to nuclear war.

SECTION 1

THE FIRST WORLD WAR

A tragic link
These deaths happened thousands of miles
and several years apart but they are
tragically linked. You will find out why in
this section.

Three fuses and one spark!

▶▶ Pages 4–9 tell you about the causes of the First World War. You will see how different factors helped to cause the war, and then try to decide which of them are long-term causes and which are short-term causes.

▼ DISCUSS

Why did European countries want to have large empires? Think about:

■ the advantages of having colonies
■ power
■ prestige.

Fuse one: Empires

In 1900, large areas of the world were controlled by European countries. The British EMPIRE, as you can see from Source 1, stretched right across the world. It was said that 'the sun never sets on the British Empire'.

A large empire was very important for trade and also for prestige. The power of a country was judged by the size of its empire. The British and French had big empires.

In the 1870s, Germany and Italy became united countries for the first time. They each wanted overseas empires, too, and a fierce competition for COLONIES developed between the countries of Europe. Colonies could bring a country great wealth in terms of raw materials for industry, cheap food and minerals such as gold and diamonds. They also provided the mother country with a market for its industrial goods.

From 1870 to 1900 there was a scramble for territory in Africa, and European countries carved up the continent between them. Germany felt that other European countries had grabbed the best of the land before it had had a chance to get any.

To be a great nation you must colonise.

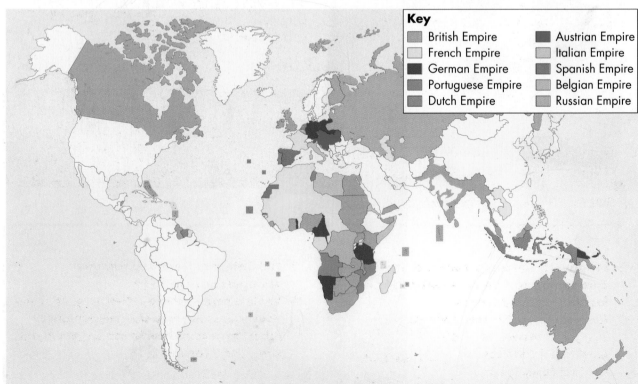

Key

British Empire	Austrian Empire
French Empire	Italian Empire
German Empire	Spanish Empire
Portuguese Empire	Belgian Empire
Dutch Empire	Russian Empire

▲ **SOURCE 1** *The world in 1900*

Fuse two: An arms race

In 1900 Britain's navy was by far the largest in the world. But Britain was worried about the growing size of the German navy. A race to build new battleships soon developed between Britain and Germany. In 1906, Britain launched a stronger and faster type of battleship called the Dreadnought. Germany quickly started to build similar ships.

Build more ships!

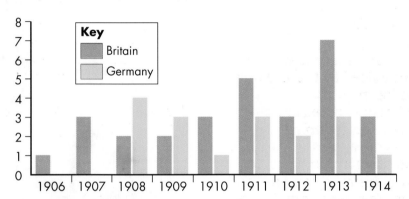

◀ **SOURCE 2** *The numbers of Dreadnoughts built by Britain and Germany, 1906–14*

Guns on rotating turrets which can fire shells over six miles in any direction

Fast modern turbine engines

Thick armour plating

▲ **SOURCE 3** *A British Dreadnought, HMS* Barham

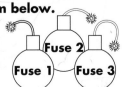

▼ ACTIVITY

1 Why were empires a source of tension in Europe? Try to sum up your answer in less than twenty words.
2 Copy the fuse diagram below. Use your answer to Question 1 to label the first fuse.

3 Did Britain or Germany have the strongest navy in 1914?
4 Write a sentence to explain why an arms race causes tension. Use this sentence to label the second fuse in the diagram you drew for Question 2.

THREE FUSES AND ONE SPARK!

Fuse three: Alliances

Before 1914, the big countries of Europe had formed two sides or ALLIANCES (see Source 4). Each member promised to help the others if there was a war.

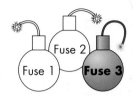

Many people thought that as long as the two alliances were equal in strength they would not risk attacking each other, and so peace would be kept. But these two 'armed camps' became more and more suspicious of each other because of the quarrels over colonies and the arms race.

▼ **ACTIVITY**

1 **Look at Source 5. Which alliance looks the strongest?**

2 **Write a sentence to explain why the alliances might increase the risk of war. Use this sentence to label the third fuse in the diagram you drew for Question 2 on page 5.**

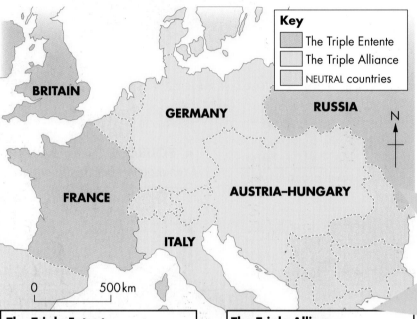

Key
- The Triple Entente
- The Triple Alliance
- NEUTRAL countries

BRITAIN
GERMANY
RUSSIA
FRANCE
AUSTRIA–HUNGARY
ITALY

N

0   500km

The Triple Entente
France and Russia promised to help each other if either was attacked, signing an agreement in 1893. Britain joined them in 1907. These countries thought Germany was getting too powerful.

The Triple Alliance
Germany had formed an alliance with Austria–Hungary and Italy. They promised to help each other if any of them had to go to war. Germany was worried it would be attacked by France or Russia.

Many countries in Europe began to expect a war. Any spark could set it off!

▲ **SOURCE 4** *A map showing the alliances in 1914*

▼ **SOURCE 5** *How Europe was divided into two armed camps*

	Germany	Austria–Hungary	Italy	Britain	France	Russia
Soldiers in the army	2,200,000	810,000	750,000	711,000	1,250,000	1,200,000
Warships	97	28	36	185	62	30
Submarines	23	62	12	64	73	9
Money spent on military preparation, 1913–14	£60 million	£22 million	£10 million	£50 million	£37 million	£67 million

The spark: Murder in Sarajevo

It is 28 June 1914 in Sarajevo, the capital of
Bosnia. Gavrilo Princip wanders the streets.
He is a member of the notorious secret society,
the Black Hand, a group of Serbian nationalists
determined to help the Serbs of Bosnia break
free from Austro-Hungarian control. He is just
one of a number of young assassins who have
come to Sarajevo to kill the heir to the Austro-
Hungarian throne, the Archduke Franz
Ferdinand. They line the route along which the
Archduke is to drive. They have bombs and
pistols ready in their pockets.

Their hatred of Austria–Hungary is fanatical. They hate the way its rulers have
oppressed and mistreated the different national groups within the Empire.
They want all Serbs to be free to live together in their own country. They want
to strike at Austria–Hungary in any way they can. And perhaps this terrorist
act will persuade the Austro–Hungarians to abandon their control of Bosnia.

Gavrilo nervously fingers the pistol in his pocket as he waits.
He also checks the phial of poison which he will swallow if he is caught.
He waits, but the Archduke does not arrive . . .

Then he hears an explosion. The deed is done. One of his
compatriots must have killed the Archduke. He slips into the
crowd in Franz Josef Street, relieved that he has not been
called upon to die for the cause.

Suddenly there is a commotion. The Archduke's
car is driving down the street towards him.
The Archduke is alive! His wife, Sophie, is sitting
in a white dress next to him. Unbelievably,
the car comes to a stop in front of Gavrilo
and the driver starts to reverse as
if he has gone the wrong way.
Gavrilo has no time to think.
He pulls his pistol from his
pocket, points it at the car and
fires. He does not know
how many times he
presses the trigger
before he is grabbed
and pushed to the
ground. Punches
and kicks rain
down on him.
It is over.

But it was far from over. Gavrilo Princip's
bullets had not only killed the
Archduke but also his wife, Sophie.
Outraged, the Austro-Hungarians wanted
revenge. This was the beginning of a chain
of events that led to the First World War.

THREE FUSES AND ONE SPARK!

How did the First World War start?

▼ **ACTIVITY A**

The cartoons on this page show the chain of events that led up to the First World War. However, they are not in the right order.

a) Work out the correct order of the events.

b) Design a flow chart to show how the war started.

28 June
The heir to the Austro-Hungarian throne, Archduke Franz Ferdinand, is assassinated in Bosnia.

The Russian army gets ready to help Serbia defend itself against the Austro-Hungarian attack.

To complete the picture, Austria declares war on Russia.

Germany, Austria's ally, sends a demand to Russia ordering it to hold back from helping Serbia.

Austria declares war on Serbia. Belgrade (in Serbia) is shelled.

Germany declares war on France and invades neutral Belgium. Britain orders Germany to withdraw from Belgium.

The Germans are still in Belgium. Britain declares war on Germany.

Germany declares war on Russia. It also begins to move its army towards France, Russia's ally.

It's Serbia that is behind this!

Austria blames Serbia for the killing of Archduke Franz Ferdinand.

The French army is put on a war footing, ready to fight a German invasion.

8

▼ ACTIVITY B

Historians are interested in *why* things happened. If they can work out why a war happened, they might be able to prevent another one. They talk about long-term causes, which build up over a long period of time and make war a possibility. They are like slow-burning fuses. They also talk about short-term causes, triggers that actually start a conflict.

RESEARCH:-
* *Why Italy & Germany have been behind other countries?*
* *How did Austro-Hungarians treat the Serbians during the assassination?*
  A.H. issued an ultimatum to Serbia. Who was willing to comply except the investigation in serbia.

→ Germany & Italy did not exist. Existed in 19th century.

1 Some of the main causes of the First World War are listed on the cards below. Some of these are long-term causes and some are short term. Make your own set of cause cards, and sort them into two piles:
   a) long-term causes
   b) short-term causes.

> Rivalry between Britain and Germany over their navies and colonies
> *long-term*

> The assassination of Archduke Franz Ferdinand
> *short-term*

> Rivalry between Austria–Hungary and Russia over the Balkans. Both empires wanted to control the Balkans
> *long term*

> The German invasion of Belgium that brought Britain into the war
> *short-term*

> The system of alliances which meant that a serious dispute between two countries might drag others into a war
> *long-term*

> The actions of the Austro-Hungarians after the assassination and the way they treated Serbia
> *short-term*

> *How did they treat them? research*

> Germany's wish to dominate Europe. Germany was very aggressive before 1914, building up its armed forces and threatening other countries
> *long-term*

> The German fear of being surrounded
> *short-term*

2 Choose one cause that you are sure is long term and one cause that you are sure is short term. Write a paragraph for each, explaining how it contributed to the start of the First World War.

▼ DISCUSS

3 Some people think that the First World War could have been avoided. What do you think? *No, never (couldn't have been avoided)*

What was life like on the Western Front?

As the German army set off for war, Kaiser Wilhelm told them that they would 'be home before the leaves have fallen from the trees'. People in Britain also expected the war to be over in a few months. But it wasn't. In fact, the two sides slugged it out for four years, along a line of trenches that stretched from the Belgian coast to the Alps. On pages 10–20 you are going to investigate why the soldiers ended up in the trenches, and what it was like for them.

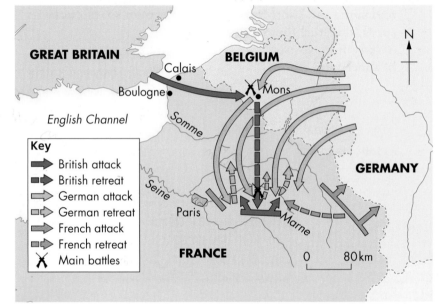

▼ **SOURCE 1** *A map showing the Battle of the Marne, September 1914*

Why did they end up in the trenches?

The Germans planned to crash through Belgium into France and defeat the French quickly before the British had a chance to cross the Channel. But the Belgian army fought bravely and held the Germans up for several weeks. The delay gave the British Expeditionary Force time to arrive and join the fighting.

The Germans made a dash for Paris. They thought the French might give up if they captured the French capital. They nearly reached their target, but the French rushed out reserve troops in buses and taxis and the Germans were stopped at the Battle of the Marne (see Source 1).

Germany then tried to capture the northern Channel ports, such as Calais and Boulogne, to prevent the British army from escaping to Britain, but the plan failed. Both sides tried unsuccessfully to break through the other's defences. By Christmas 1914 the two sides had fought to a standstill along the line shown in Source 2. Both sides dug trenches to protect themselves from machine-gun fire and heavy artillery shells. Neither side was able to advance. Neither side was prepared to give up. There was a STALEMATE on the Western Front.

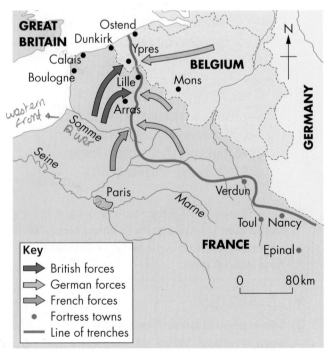

▲ **SOURCE 2** *The line of trenches in December 1914*

Joining up and kitting out

Young men in Britain rushed to join the army as soon as war was declared. Most people felt that the war would be over by Christmas and were anxious to get involved before it was too late. Soldiers came from all classes of society and from all regions of Britain and its empire. Indians, Australians, Canadians, New Zealanders and West Indians offered to serve on the Western Front.

service cap and regimental cap badge

Mark II Lee Enfield Rifle

large canvas pack for carrying woolly cap, spare socks and greatcoat

digging tool – handle and head separate

150 rounds of ammunition in belt and pouches

full water bottle and carrier

two canvas bags to carry a respirator and a gas mask

haversack for carrying rations, paybook, toothbrush, soap and towel, spare bootlaces, mess tin (to eat from) and cover, fork and spoon, mending and darning kit

bayonet (a blade that could be attached to the end of the rifle)

identity tag

▲ **SOURCE 3** *A soldier leaving for France and a list of the kit he would have carried with him*

▼ **ACTIVITY**

We are going to follow one young army recruit, John Everyman. He is not a real person, but everything he does is based on real events.

As you work through pages 11–20, make notes about what happens to John. You could divide your notes up by using the same headings as we have done.

Later, using the sources and your notes, you will *either*:

a) write several diary extracts or letters home from John. These should describe his experiences between 1915 and 1918

or:

b) conduct an imaginary interview with John for a film documentary. You will make up the questions and John's answers.

Joining up and kitting out

John Everyman (see the Activity above) joined up with other young men from his part of the country in a PALS REGIMENT.

The new recruits were sent for training. They had to wait several weeks for their equipment. They spent a lot of time marching around the parade ground using wooden sticks in place of real rifles. Sometimes the training was very hard.

Source 3 shows what John's kit was like.

WHAT WAS LIFE LIKE ON THE WESTERN FRONT?

To France

John's REGIMENT crossed the English Channel at night, in open boats, and arrived at Le Havre in France. It was not a pleasant crossing and most of the men were glad to reach dry land. They were sent to a temporary camp for further training, but it was not long before they were sent to the FRONT LINE.

John found himself in a system of trenches, which stretched for miles and miles in all directions. Behind the front-line trenches there were support trenches, with communication trenches joining the two so that the soldiers could move around. There were also dead-end trenches to confuse the enemy, and large DUGOUTS.

Generally, each COMPANY of 240 soldiers was supposed to spend six days per month in the front-line trenches. But, as John was to find out, six days could turn into weeks or even months – if you survived.

▼ **ACTIVITY**

Make some notes on John's journey to the trenches.

Jo France

▼ **SOURCE 4** *Written in 1973 by the novelist Henry Williamson, who went to France in 1914*

We landed at Le Havre and after one night in a rest camp found ourselves in a series of trucks.

At St Omer we marched to a convent, where we practised advances in formation across old stubble, and rumours said we were 'for it'. That night six of us stood among the trees of the garden and watched flickerings in the faraway eastern sky and heard the boom of heavy guns.

Next morning we marched along a straight road between rows of elms and so to Wipers [the British soldiers' name for Ypres]. We slept that night in the cloth hall.

In the morning the bugles sounded the alarm . . . Up the Menin Road we marched when coming towards us were prams holding silent children, wounded soldiers, refugees with sacks filled with dead chickens and 40 tall soldiers with staring eyes and hollow cheeks.

We were not needed [at the front] and returned to Ypres . . . and marching south found ourselves in a large wood of oaks. There we remained interested and content for the weather was warm. We slept in bunkers made of oak posts and sandbags.

▲ **SOURCE 5** *The road from Menin to Ypres, the main route to the front-line trenches at Ypres, in 1917*

▲ **SOURCE 6** *The Worcestershire Regiment going into action, 28 June 1916*

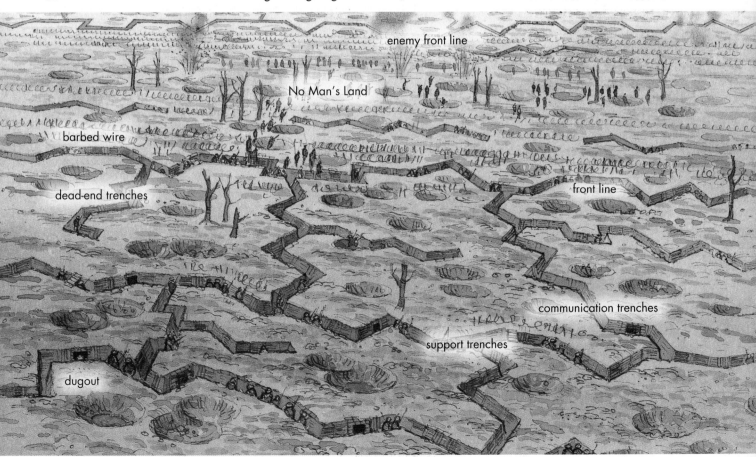

enemy front line

No Man's Land

barbed wire

dead-end trenches

front line

communication trenches

support trenches

dugout

▲ **SOURCE 7** *The trench system*

WHAT WAS LIFE LIKE ON THE WESTERN FRONT?

In the trenches

Life in the trenches was a peculiar mixture of boredom and uncertainty, of discomfort and danger. For much of the time shells were falling. Soldiers lived with the ever-present fear of being killed by an exploding shell, a sniper's bullet or a poison gas attack which would burn their lungs and choke them to death. John was glad to have his friends around him. They all helped each other through the difficult times.

The front-line trenches were most active at night, because an attack was most likely after dark. Sentries had to keep a careful watch, and scouting parties were sent out to capture prisoners, spy on the enemy and repair the barbed wire barricades.

Not all parts of the front line were dangerous. There was little fighting in some areas and the enemy was rarely seen. In such places, soldiers often enjoyed the comradeship and new experiences that life in the army brought.

Soldiers had to cope with extremes of weather. Heavy rain could leave the trenches knee deep with freezing water. Then, in the summer, the sun could bake the soldiers in blistering heat.

John experienced danger and near death, followed by long periods of quiet. When he got bored he smoked, played cards or carried out routine duties such as filling sandbags, cleaning latrines or fetching supplies.

▼ **SOURCE 8** *An artist's view of a trench*

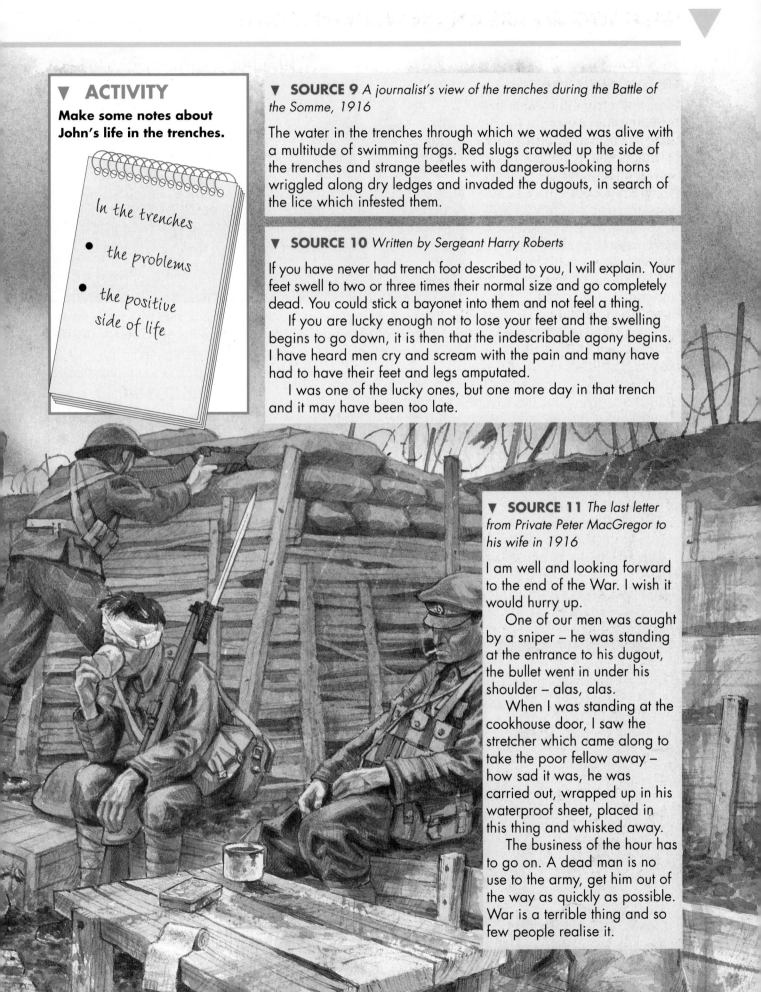

▼ **ACTIVITY**

Make some notes about John's life in the trenches.

In the trenches

- the problems
- the positive side of life

▼ **SOURCE 9** *A journalist's view of the trenches during the Battle of the Somme, 1916*

The water in the trenches through which we waded was alive with a multitude of swimming frogs. Red slugs crawled up the side of the trenches and strange beetles with dangerous-looking horns wriggled along dry ledges and invaded the dugouts, in search of the lice which infested them.

▼ **SOURCE 10** *Written by Sergeant Harry Roberts*

If you have never had trench foot described to you, I will explain. Your feet swell to two or three times their normal size and go completely dead. You could stick a bayonet into them and not feel a thing.

If you are lucky enough not to lose your feet and the swelling begins to go down, it is then that the indescribable agony begins. I have heard men cry and scream with the pain and many have had to have their feet and legs amputated.

I was one of the lucky ones, but one more day in that trench and it may have been too late.

▼ **SOURCE 11** *The last letter from Private Peter MacGregor to his wife in 1916*

I am well and looking forward to the end of the War. I wish it would hurry up.

One of our men was caught by a sniper – he was standing at the entrance to his dugout, the bullet went in under his shoulder – alas, alas.

When I was standing at the cookhouse door, I saw the stretcher which came along to take the poor fellow away – how sad it was, he was carried out, wrapped up in his waterproof sheet, placed in this thing and whisked away.

The business of the hour has to go on. A dead man is no use to the army, get him out of the way as quickly as possible. War is a terrible thing and so few people realise it.

Going over the top

Eventually, the time came for John and his comrades to go 'over the top', to attack the Germans across the land between the trenches called No Man's Land. This was a desolate area. There was no vegetation. It was covered with massive barbed wire barriers. There were huge shell craters.

First, the ARTILLERY bombarded the enemy trenches with shells to try to clear them out before the attack. Of course, it also warned the enemy that an attack was coming. John crouched in the trench waiting for the whistle to blow, then he and his friends climbed over and ran across the broken ground in a great human wave, all the while waiting for the enemy's machine guns to open fire.

Looking back these attacks often seem pointless. They rarely gained more than a few metres of ground. Machine-gun fire could mow down attacking soldiers in their hundreds. In one day at the Battle of the Somme, the British suffered 57,000 casualties, 20,000 of whom died.

One of the worst battles of the First World War took place in 1917 at Passchendaele. Before the first attack the land was drenched by heavy rain and the battleground had been churned to mud by shells and previous attacks. It was not unheard of for groups of men and horses to be swallowed up, drowning in the mud before anyone could reach them.

▲ **SOURCE 12** *Men going over the top. This is a still from a film made by the British government in 1916 called* The Battle of the Somme. *It was shown to millions of people in cinemas all over Britain*

▼ **DISCUSS**

1 Look at Sources 12, 13 and 14. Which do you think is most useful to the historian wanting to know what it was like to go over the top?

2 Source 12 was 'staged'. It does not show an actual attack. Does this change your answer to Question 1?

► **SOURCE 13**
A picture from the Illustrated London News of 29 July 1916. It shows men from the East Surrey Regiment kicking a football as they launch an attack

'THE SURREYS PLAY THE GAME!' KICKING FOOTBALLS TOWARDS THE GERMAN TRENCHES UNDER A HAIL OF SHELLS.

▲ **SOURCE 14** Over the Top, a painting by John Nash. Nash served in France from November 1916 to January 1918 when he was made an official war artist

The first line seemed to go on without end, from left to right. A second line, then a third and fourth followed the first line. They came on at a steady pace, as if expecting to find nothing alive in our front trenches. A few seconds later, the rattle of machine-gun fire broke out from our whole line. Whole sections appeared to fall. All along the line, Englishmen could be seen throwing their arms into the air and collapsing, never to move again . . . while other casualties crawled into shell holes for shelter . . . With all this were mingled the moans of the wounded, cries for help and the last screams of death. Again and again the lines of British infantry broke against the German defences like waves against a cliff, only to be beaten back. It was an amazing sight of great bravery.

▼ **SOURCE 15** *Written by Private Henry Russell about the Battle of the Somme in 1916*

During our advance, I saw many of my colleagues killed by German machine-gun fire, but this somehow or other did not seem to worry me and I continued to go forward until I suddenly became aware that there were few of us left capable of going on.

I found myself in the company of an officer, Lieutenant Wallace. We dived into a flat, shallow hole made by our guns, not knowing what to do next . . . I came to the conclusion that going on would be suicidal and that the best thing we could do would be to stay there and try to pick off any Germans who might expose themselves. Lieutenant Wallace said, however, that we had been ordered to go on at all costs and that we must comply with this order. At this, he stood up and within seconds dropped down riddled with bullets. This left me with the same problem and having observed his action, I felt that I must do the same. I stood up and was immediately hit by two bullets and dropped down . . .

I am now convinced that when it comes to the crunch, nobody has any fear at all.

▼ **ACTIVITY**

Make some notes about going over the top.

Going over the top

Wounded

John Everyman was horrified to see so many of his friends die. Half of his regiment was killed or injured at the Battle of the Somme. Several of the men who had joined with him, his pals, had been killed by shell and machine-gun fire. He himself was wounded in the shoulder. His best friend, Bert, dragged him off the battlefield to receive treatment.

Wounded soldiers often depended on the bravery of their friends to get them back to their own trenches. Many died in No Man's Land because there was no one to help them.

Behind the lines

Back behind the front-line trenches there were makeshift hospitals and DRESSING STATIONS where the wounded were tended.

Many women worked in these hospitals. They belonged to the Voluntary Aid Detachments and the First Aid Nursing Auxiliary. As the war went on, and more and more men were needed to fight, the generals decided that women could do other jobs in the army like cooking, typing and nursing which previously men had done. So, in 1917, the Woman's Army Auxiliary Corps was set up.

▼ **SOURCE 17** *From Baroness Elizabeth de T'Serclaes' autobiography*

We slept in our clothes and cut our hair short so that it would tuck inside our caps. Dressing meant simply putting on our boots . . . There were times when we had to scrape the lice off with the blunt edge of a knife and our underclothes stuck to us.

▼ **SOURCE 18** *From a book about women in the war by modern historian, Roy Terry*

On 30 May 1918, eight women were killed in a raid on Camp 1 at Abbeville in Northern France. Seven others were wounded, one of whom died later. The bravery of the survivors earned commendations from all and three military medals were awarded to the women who helped in the rescue . . .

▼ **SOURCE 19** *Gassed by John Singer Sargent*

► **SOURCE 20** *Mairi Chisholm and Elizabeth de T'Serclaes, driving an ambulance through the ruins of a French town in 1917. Both had joined the First Aid Nursing Auxiliary*

▼ **ACTIVITY**

Make some more notes describing what John did, who he met and what he saw when he was 'behind the lines'.

Behind the lines

Winning the war

John recovered from his wounds. In the spring of 1918 John and Bert were back in the trenches and facing a fierce German attack. German 'stormtroopers' crashed through their defences. Things were going very badly. But the German advance ground to a halt. In May, American troops arrived. The Americans were fresh and eager to fight, and brought lots of weapons and supplies with them.

Also, the British had a new weapon – the tank. John had heard of it before but had never seen one of the monsters in action ... until now. The Allies began pushing the Germans back all along the front line. For the first time John and Bert thought they might make it through the war. They nearly did, but just before the ARMISTICE, on 11 November, Bert was killed. John was angry and bitter at this last piece of cruel bad luck. Now all he wanted to do was get back home.

▼ **SOURCE 21** *From '1914 – The Soldier' by Rupert Brooke (1887–1915). Brooke died in Greece on his way to fight in Turkey; he never actually saw any fighting*

If I should die, think only this of me:
That there's some corner of a foreign field
That is forever England. There shall be
In that rich earth a richer dust concealed;
A dust whom England bore, shaped, made aware,
Gave, once, her flowers to love, her ways to roam,
A body of England's, breathing English air,
Washed by the rivers, blest by suns of home ...

▼ **SOURCE 22** *From 'Dulce et Decorum Est', written in 1917 by Wilfred Owen (1893–1918). Owen was badly injured in 1917 but went back to fight. He was killed on the Western Front three days before Armistice Day in 1918. In this poem he describes a poison gas attack*

If in some smothering dreams, you too could pace
Behind the wagon that we flung him in ...
If you could hear, at every jolt, the blood
Come gargling from the froth-corrupted lungs,
Obscene as cancer, bitter as the cud
Of vile, incurable sores on innocent tongues, –
My friend, you would not tell with such high zest
To children ardent for some desperate glory,
The old Lie: *Dulce et decorum est*
Pro patria mori.
[It is sweet and proper to die for your country]

▼ **DISCUSS**

1 How do the poems in Sources 21 and 22 differ in their view of the war?

2 Why do you think they differ so much?

▼ **ACTIVITY**

3 Make your last set of notes describing John's attitudes and feelings at the end of the war.

Winning the war

4 Now use your notes to write the diary extracts, letters, or the transcript of an interview with John (see the Activity on page 11).

You could also carry out your own research to add more details to your work.

▼ **REVIEW ACTIVITY**

5 Look back to the pictures on page 3. Write a paragraph to explain the link between these two deaths.

SECTION 2

THE RISE OF THE DICTATORS AND THE CAUSES OF THE SECOND WORLD WAR

Mussolini

Stalin

Hitler

Three dictators

After the First World War many parts of Europe were in a mess. There was violence and unemployment.

Many countries turned to dictators to guide them through these difficult times.

In this section you will find out why. You will study Nazi Germany in more depth, to understand what it was like to live in a dictatorship. Finally, you will consider the role of one dictator, Hitler, in causing the Second World War.

Was Germany treated fairly after the First World War?

It is 1919. You are at Versailles, near Paris. The great powers have come together to draw up a peace treaty to end the war. Top of the agenda is how to deal with Germany. On pages 22–25 you will decide how the Germans should be treated and then compare your ideas with what actually happened.

The aims of the Big Three

Most of the decisions will be made by the 'Big Three' – the USA, France and Britain. The Germans are not allowed to join in the discussions. The leaders of the Big Three have different aims:

The USA

Germany must be treated fairly!

The USA has suffered much less than Europe during the war. **Woodrow Wilson**, the American President, wants lasting peace in Europe. He believes that punishing Germany too harshly will only result in the Germans wanting revenge later on. He wants to agree a fair peace treaty that will not lead to trouble in the future. He believes that different national groups, such as the Poles and the Czechs, should run their own affairs and be strong independent countries.

Britain

Germany must be punished!

The British leader, **Lloyd George**, wants a fair settlement. He does not want the Germans to feel hard done by and become aggressive and vengeful in the future. However, the British people are demanding that Germany is punished harshly. A popular phrase in the British press is: 'Squeeze Germany till the pips squeak'. Lloyd George cannot ignore these feelings.

France

Germany must be crippled!

France, led by **Georges Clemenceau**, wants revenge. Much of the war has taken place in France. The damage has been staggering: over 75,000 homes and 23,000 factories have been destroyed, and the land in the battle zones has been ripped apart. One and a half million French soldiers have died. Clemenceau wants to punish Germany and he wants COMPENSATION. He also wants to make sure that France is safe from future attacks.

What will you decide?

▼ **ACTIVITY**

1 **Get into groups of three. One of you should represent France, one of you Britain and one of you the USA.**
   a) **Read the aims of your country carefully (see page 22).**
   b) **Look at the cards below and decide on one solution for each question. Try to reach a decision that you can all agree about. This is called a 'unanimous' decision. If you can't all agree, take a vote to decide. This is called a 'split' decision.**

---

1 What do you do about the German army?
a) Disband the German army altogether   *France*
b) Allow the army to remain strong to defend Europe from the COMMUNIST threat in the East   *G B*
c) Cut the army down to about 100,000 men, but forbid the Germans to build any tanks   *U.S.A.*

2 What do you do about the navy and the airforce?
a) Do not allow the Germans to have any ships or aeroplanes   *France*
b) Allow them a few ships, but no aeroplanes   *G. B.*
c) Allow them to keep most of their ships and planes   *U.S.A.*

3 Who will pay for the damage caused by the war?
a) Make the Germans pay a huge amount of money in REPARATIONS for the damage and destruction caused by the war   *France*
b) Make them pay a moderate amount, enough to punish them for the war damage but not enough to cause them terrible economic problems   *G. B.*
c) Make them pay a small amount. Germany is in a poor economic state and you don't want to make things worse   *U.S.A.*

4 Who should be blamed for the war?
a) Make Germany accept all the blame for starting the war   *France*
b) Accept that several countries are equally responsible for starting the war   *U.S.A*
c) Make Germany accept most of the blame   *G. B.*

5 What do you do about Germany's overseas empire?
a) Let Germany keep its colonies   *U.S.A*
b) Take away all Germany's colonies and give them to the Allies   *France*
c) Let Germany keep some colonies but give important ones to the Allies   *G. B.*

6 What should you do about the Rhineland (an area in Germany which borders France)?
a) Nothing. Leave things as they are   *U.S.A*
b) Forbid the Germans to build any new fortifications in the Rhineland   *G.B.*
c) Demilitarise the Rhineland. Do not allow the Germans to station any troops there   *France*

7 Should Alsace-Lorraine be taken away from Germany?
Alsace-Lorraine was French until 1870. It has been German since then. Most of the people there speak French. Should you give Alsace-Lorraine back to France?
a) Yes, give it to France   *France*
b) No, let Germany keep it   *U.S.A.*
c) Ask the people of Alsace-Lorraine to vote on whether to be in France or Germany   *G. B*

---

   c) **Record your decisions using a table like this:**

Decision	Our choice	Unanimous or split decision	Reasons for choice

2 **Discuss with the whole class what you decided.**

What did the Germans think of the Treaty of Versailles?

The peace treaty with Germany was called the Treaty of Versailles. It was signed on 28 June 1919. Source 1 tells you the main points. How do they compare with your decisions from the Activity on page 23? The German government thought the terms of the treaty were very unfair. They had made harsh treaties in the past when they had won wars, but they believed this treaty was unacceptable.

- They did not feel they should take all the blame for starting the war.
- They were horrified by the huge reparations they had to pay. The German economy was already in a terrible mess. They felt the Treaty would stop them recovering.
- They felt humiliated by losing German land and colonies.
- They felt bitter about the fact that they had to disarm when the other countries did not.

But Germany had to sign or the war would start up again. You can see some of the reactions to the Treaty in Sources 3–5.

know 4 Exam

▼ **SOURCE 1** *The terms of the Treaty of Versailles*

1 Germany was to accept the blame for starting the war, under the terms of the 'War guilt' clause. *To punish Germany & get revenge.*
2 Germany was to reduce its army to 100,000 men. *To weaken Germany so that it could not threaten Europe again*
3 Germany could only have six battleships in its navy. *B*
4 Germany was not allowed to build any aeroplanes, submarines or tanks. *B*
5 Germany had to pay £6,600 million in reparations to the countries that had won the war. *C*
6 All Germany's colonies were given to France, Britain and other countries. *C*
7 Germany was forbidden to unite with Austria. *B*
8 Germany was to demilitarise the Rhineland. *B*
9 Alsace-Lorraine went back to France. *C*
10 Germany also lost a strip of land called the Polish Corridor. This was given to Poland, cutting East Prussia off from the rest of Germany. *A*

▲ **SOURCE 2** *Europe after the Treaty of Versailles. There were three other treaties: one for each of Germany's allies. In one treaty the Austro-Hungarian Empire was broken up into independent states*

▲ **SOURCE 3** *A German cartoon showing the Devil and his cronies gloating over the Treaty of Versailles. The figures are called Greed, Revenge and Lust for Power*

The 6 Devils are Lust (lust a power

▲ **SOURCE 4** *A German cartoon published in 1919. The German mother is saying to her child, 'When we have paid 100,000,000,000 marks, then I shall be able to give you something to eat'*

▼ **SOURCE 5** *From the German newspaper* Deutsche Zeitung *on the day the Treaty was signed*

Deutsche Zeitung

28 June, 1919

PRIMARY
RELISTIC
REVENGE

Today in the Hall of Mirrors of Versailles the disgraceful Treaty is being signed. Do not forget it! The German people will, with unceasing labour, press forward to reconquer the place among the nations to which it is entitled. Then will come revenge for the shame of 1919.

▼ **ACTIVITY A**

1 For each of the terms of the Treaty shown in Source 1, say whether you think its main aim was:

A ■ to punish Germany and get revenge

B ■ to weaken Germany so that it could not threaten Europe again

C ■ to reward or compensate the Allies.

Explain your choice for each one.

▼ **DISCUSS**

2 Do you think the terms of the Treaty were too harsh on Germany, or not harsh enough?

3 What does Source 5 suggest that the consequences of the Treaty might be in Germany?

▼ **ACTIVITY B**

4 a) Write a letter to a German newspaper condemning the Treaty and explaining why the terms are unfair to Germany. You could use Sources 3–5 for ideas.

expressing strong disapproval

formal 1919

b) Write a reply from a French person saying why Germany deserves to be treated like this. You could refer to page 22 for ideas.

▲ **25**

The rise of the dictators

The words 'dictatorship' and 'democracy' are important to your understanding of twentieth-century history. The aim of pages 26–27 is to make clear what the two words mean.

▼ **ACTIVITY**

Work in pairs or groups.

1 Copy the table below and sort statements 3–11 into the appropriate column. If there are any that you find difficult to place, put them aside.

In a democracy . . . *a group*	In a dictatorship . . . *one person*
1 Everybody can vote and help to choose the government	**2** There are no free elections to change the government
8, 10, 11, 7, 3	4, 6, 5, 9

3 Everybody, including the government, must obey the laws of the land

4 The government controls the media – newspapers, radio and films – allowing people to see and hear only what it wants them to

5 People who criticise the government may be tortured, imprisoned or sent to special camps

6 Secret police keep the people under control, often using brutal methods like torture

7 People have the freedom to criticise the government and protest about its policies

8 People can follow any religion they wish

9 Trade unions are banned

10 Newspapers can write what they like about the government

11 A government has a limited time in power, after which voters can choose a different government

2 Study the information on page 27. Does it help you with any of the statements you couldn't place? Does it make you want to change anything? Have another look at your table and rearrange the statements if you need to.

Fascist and Communist dictatorships

The USA, Britain and France remained democracies after the upheaval of the First World War, but many other powerful countries rejected democracy and became dictatorships in the 1930s.

▼ **SOURCE 1** *Europe between the wars*

Germany

In the 1920s, after the Kaiser had fled, Germany experimented with democracy. After a very difficult start, the new democratic REPUBLIC seemed to be doing quite well. But, in 1929, it was hit by a terrible DEPRESSION. This resulted in growing support for the Nazi Party, led by Adolf Hitler. In 1933, Hitler became Chancellor of Germany and set about establishing a FASCIST dictatorship. You can find out about life in Nazi Germany on pages 36–45.

Italy

Italy was in a desperate state after the First World War. There was a high level of unemployment, strikes and demonstrations were taking place, food prices were high and people were hungry. Violence erupted in the streets as rival political groups fought each other. Many Italians were worried that there might be a Communist revolution like in Russia. The government seemed unable to control the violence or do anything about the country's problems.

Benito Mussolini, the leader of the Fascist Party, said he would bring order to the streets and provide a stable government. In 1922 Mussolini was made Prime Minister, after thousands of Fascists marched on Rome in support of him. Mussolini set about building a Fascist dictatorship. He quickly dealt with his opponents. They were beaten up, murdered or imprisoned by his secret police. Other political parties were abolished. Workers were not allowed to go on strike. The Fascist Party ran all the newspapers and nobody was allowed to criticise the government. Mussolini did bring back order and, at first, he created more jobs, improved Italy's transport system and helped farmers to produce more food.

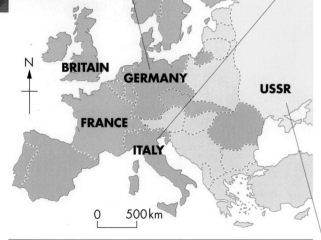

Key

▨ Fascist dictatorships	▢ Communist dictatorships
▢ Other dictatorships	▨ Democracies

USSR

The Russian Empire was replaced by a COMMUNIST dictatorship in October 1917. It was ruled first by Lenin and then by Stalin. It was the world's first Communist state and represented an experiment in a new way of organising society. It was called the Union of Soviet Socialist Republics – the USSR. You can find out more about it on pages 28–31.

▼ DISCUSS

Why might people think dictatorships can solve problems like violence, unemployment, strikes and food shortages better than democracies?

Why were people in the West so frightened of Communism?

In 1917 the Russian Revolution put a Communist government in power in Russia. Some historians say that it was the most important event of the twentieth century. Certainly, between 1917 and 1991 (when Communism in Russia collapsed), people in Western Europe, the USA and other parts of the world were terrified that Communist ideas might spread to their country. On pages 28–31 you are going to find out why they were so afraid.

He was against capitalism.
• Communism collapsed only in USSR and East countries.
• Not everywhere.

What is Communism?

The man who developed the idea of Communism was Karl Marx. He studied what was happening in Europe and he thought this unjust system could not last.

The world is controlled by CAPITALISTS, who own the factories and banks and make large profits. They pay their workers low wages and spend nothing on making working conditions pleasant.

Eventually the workers will not accept this unjust situation any longer. There will be a revolution. The workers will rise up and seize power for themselves. Then, a workers' government will share out the wealth of society fairly.

This will lead to a Communist society:

- people will co-operate with each other and share things
- people will work at what they are good at
- everybody will take what they need from a central pool of resources
- machines will do a lot of the work so people will have free time to enjoy life.

Karl Marx

How did the Communists take power in Russia?

Marx's ideas were all theoretical. This process had never actually been tried anywhere … yet!

Marx died in 1883, but he had written lots of books and many people read about and believed in his ideas. They were called Marxists. One of these was a Russian called Lenin. He thought Russia was ripe for a revolution, just like Marx had described.

The vast Russian Empire was ruled by Tsar (Emperor) Nicholas. It was a backward country. Most of the people were poor peasant farmers who lived hard lives.

The workers in factories and mines were very badly paid and worked and lived in dreadful conditions. The Tsar kept control by force, using harsh laws, spies and secret police.

The First World War had made the situation worse. Nearly two million soldiers had been killed. There was a severe shortage of food and fuel. People were starving. The Tsar was forced to give up his throne and, in the confusion that followed, Lenin seized power in the name of the workers. The world's first Communist state was born.

How did the Communists change Russia?

> Titles and ranks have been dropped. Everybody is called 'tovaritsch' (comrade).

> Houses have been taken from their rich owners and shared among the workers. One owner of a palace now lives in his bathroom!

> Women are equal to men.

> People who were powerful and rich before the Revolution are now known as 'former people'. The wealth of 'former people' has been confiscated by the state. 'Former people' cannot work so they have been forced to sell their belongings to pay for food.

> The workers have been told to take control of their factories and to run them by committees.

> The peasants have been told to share out the land between themselves.

Lenin

> The state (government) has taken control of the banks.

> All newspapers, except Communist ones, are banned.

> No political parties are allowed, except the Communist Party.

▼ ACTIVITY

1 The speech bubbles around Karl Marx (page 28) show what he thought a Communist society would be like. The bubbles around Lenin (above) show what actually happened in the first ten years of Communist rule in Russia. What do you think of Communism so far? Copy the table below and write as many points from pages 28–29 as you can under each heading. This is asking you to express *your* point of view based on what you have read.

Good Communist ideas	Bad Communist ideas

▼ DISCUSS

2 Now think about Communism from the point of view of people at the time. Why might:
   a) a factory owner in Britain
   b) a factory worker in Britain
   like or dislike Communism?

▲ 29

Stalin's dictatorship

Lenin was a ruthless leader. He led Russia through civil war, famine and hardship. He died in 1924. He was succeeded by Joseph Stalin.

Russia was now called the USSR or 'the SOVIET Union'. Stalin wanted to turn the Soviet Union into a great power, which would show the world how good Communism was. He wanted to turn it into a modern, industrial country. He wanted to catch up with the powerful countries in the West, like the USA and Britain. And he wanted to build the weapons he needed to protect his country.

In the 1930s, some people thought he was doing a good job; others, who knew what was going on behind the scenes, weren't so sure.

Features of Stalin's Communist dictatorship

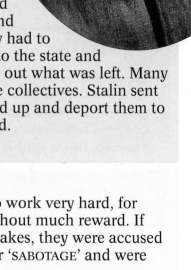

State-controlled industry

All the main industries were run by the government. Each industry was set targets that it had to reach in five years. Some of these targets were almost impossible because there was a shortage of raw materials. But the results were amazing. Over 1,500 massive new factories and 100 new industrial towns were built during the first Five-Year Plan.

Collective farming

Peasants were forced to hand over their land, animals and tools to a collective farm and work CO-OPERATIVELY. They had to give a lot of their produce to the state and were then allowed to share out what was left. Many peasants refused to join the collectives. Stalin sent police and soldiers to round up and deport them to labour camps. Millions died.

The workers

Workers had to work very hard, for long hours, without much reward. If they made mistakes, they were accused of 'wrecking' or 'SABOTAGE' and were arrested.

Even so, many workers supported Stalin because they thought he was building a better future for them.

Terror

Stalin had a huge secret police force, which had spies and informers everywhere. Children were even encouraged to inform on their parents!

Anyone who opposed or criticised Stalin was arrested, tortured, and either executed or sent to a labour camp. Stalin used the prisoners from the labour camps to dig canals and cut timber in the frozen north where no one else would work.

The purges

Stalin 'purged' all the people in the Communist Party who might challenge his leadership. They were arrested and put on trial in public. At these great 'show trials' people were forced to confess to all sorts of crimes before they were sentenced and executed.

Control of ideas

The state controlled all newspapers, books, films and radio programmes. The Russian people only received the information Stalin wanted them to receive. Churches were closed and religion was banned in many places because the Communists did not believe in God. School books were re-written to show children how great Stalin and the Communist system was.

Leadership cult

There were statues and paintings of Stalin everywhere. Propaganda, films and posters were designed to convince people that Stalin was the best person to guide them to a wonderful Communist future. For example, this poster shows Stalin marching alongside miners, as a supportive comrade. It was designed during the first Five-Year Plan.

▼ **ACTIVITY**

1 Add new 'good ideas' and 'bad ideas' to the table you created on page 29.
2 Look at the following list of people, who all live in non-Communist countries. Think about which of them might be afraid of Communism spreading to their country and why.

   ■ A rich landowner
   ■ A Christian priest
   ■ A worker in a steel factory
   ■ An industrialist who owns several factories
   ■ A poor farm labourer
   ■ A middle-class doctor
   ■ A teacher
   ■ The owner of a newspaper

3 Write a sentence to explain why the people you have chosen would be afraid of Communism:

   ... would be frightened of Communism spreading to their country because ...

Why did the Germans vote for Adolf Hitler?

> **Adolf Hitler became Chancellor of Germany in 1933. He also became one of the most hated figures of the twentieth century. But he did not seize power. He was voted into power. On pages 32–35 you will examine why this happened.**

After Germany was defeated in the First World War, it became a democratic republic called the Weimar Republic. Its citizens could:

- vote in elections to choose who should run Germany
- hold meetings and form trade unions
- say what they believed in and read what they chose
- only be arrested if they broke the law.

The new republic had a difficult beginning. Its leaders were blamed for signing the hated Treaty of Versailles (see page 24). There was high unemployment and many people were poor and hungry. The Communists tried to seize power just as they had in Russia (see page 28) and there was fighting in the streets.

The situation got much worse in 1923. Hyperinflation meant that people needed more and more money to buy the same amount of things.

Look at Source 2. At the start of 1923, this much money might have bought a row of houses. In November 1923, you would have needed 200 of these notes to buy a loaf of bread. Middle-class people who had money in the bank found their savings were worthless.

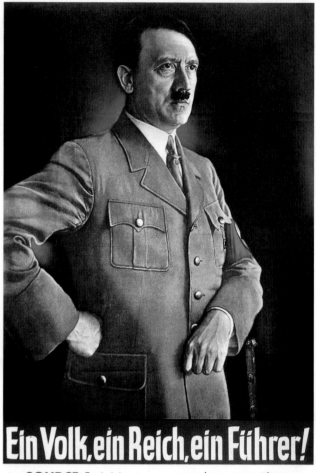

▲ **SOURCE 1** A Nazi propaganda poster. The caption reads, 'One People, one Empire, one Leader'

▲ **SOURCE 2** A one billion mark bank note from November 1923

Adolf Hitler: the early years

Adolf Hitler was born in Austria in 1889. He was a complete failure at school. He hated his father, and worshipped his mother. It seems that his father, who was often drunk, treated him badly.

Vienna

Both his mother and his father were dead by the time Hitler was 18 and he went off to Vienna to try his luck. He earned a living doing odd jobs. He may have developed his hatred of Jews in Vienna where, poor and miserable himself, he saw rich Jews running big department stores and other successful businesses. He was an outsider.

The First World War

Hitler's fortunes totally changed in the army. He found warmth and comradeship in the trenches of the First World War. He won medals for bravery and fought hard, until he was badly gassed in 1918. Germany's defeat left him bitter. He blamed the leaders of the Weimar Republic who he said were all Jews and Communists. He said that they had 'stabbed the German army in the back' by agreeing to surrender.

The Nazi Party

Back in Germany, Hitler helped to form the new Nazi Party – Fascists who opposed the Communists. He was a great speaker. He seemed to have power over the people listening to him. But he did not believe in elections. He thought the Nazis should seize power by force.

He tried to seize power in 1923, but he failed and ended up in prison. There he wrote down his ideas in a book called *Mein Kampf* (My Struggle), which became a bestseller. After he was released he started to build up the Nazi Party, but he received little support.

Most people thought Hitler's Nazi Party was a group of vicious thugs and Hitler himself a joke. And besides, by 1925, Germany was through the bad times. The economy was back on the rails. Reparations had been rearranged. Germany had even been invited to join the international club, the League of Nations.

Elections

Hitler decided to change his policy. The Nazis would compete in elections and gain power democratically. Then, and only then, would he smash democracy and set up a dictatorship.

But the Nazis did not do very well in elections either. In 1928 they were still the smallest party. Only 2.6% of Germans voted for the Nazi Party.

▼ **SOURCE 3** *Some of the main ideas contained in Hiler's* Mein Kampf, *1924*

24 points

- The Treaty of Versailles must be cancelled and land taken from Germany must be returned. *To abolish the treaty of Versailles.*
- People of German blood in Czechoslovakia and Austria must be allowed to live in a Greater Germany.
- We demand land and colonies to feed our people and to house surplus population.
- We demand a strong central government led by a single strong leader, a 'Führer'.
- The Germans are the 'Master Race'. They must keep themselves pure. Only those of German blood may be citizens. No Jews may be members of the nation.

▼ **ACTIVITY**

1 Read Source 3 carefully. Choose three Nazi ideas which you think many Germans might have approved of. Complete a chart like this to explain your choice.

24 points program

Idea in *Mein Kampf*	Why people in Germany might have liked it
Abolish the treaty of Versailles	Reparation, territories, colonies will be given up leaving space.

2 List the reasons why Adolf Hitler and the Nazis were not successful up to 1928.

WHY DID THE GERMANS VOTE FOR ADOLF HITLER?

The Great Depression: Hitler's big chance!

In 1929, the Great Depression struck. It started in the USA. The STOCK MARKET suddenly crashed and businesses went BANKRUPT. This affected other countries because the USA stopped buying foreign goods and stopped lending money to other countries. Millions of people all over the world lost their jobs.

The Great Depression hit Germany particularly hard because it relied on huge loans of money from the USA:

- German companies collapsed
- the unemployment rate soared
- there was violence on the streets
- farming also hit a crisis because of low food prices.

But disaster for Germany was good news for Hitler. He organised the Nazi Party like an army. He made speeches blaming the weak government for the crisis. He also blamed Communists and Jews. Hitler said that only the Nazis could re-establish law and order in Germany. Many Nazis became stormtroopers, called the SA or brownshirts because of the uniform that they wore. They organised big rallies to celebrate the Nazi cause. Many unemployed men joined the SA. It gave them hope and purpose. They beat up political opponents of the Nazi Party, particularly Communists.

As the economic problems got worse, the Nazis got more votes in each election. In 1932, the Nazi Party won the highest number of seats in the Reichstag, the German parliament. In 1933, Hitler was made Chancellor of Germany. The Nazis were now in charge of Germany.

▼ ACTIVITY

Sources 4–7 suggest reasons why people voted for Hitler. Look at the characters below. Why do you think each one might have voted for Hitler?

Gunther Hofer: unemployed

> I fought bravely in the First World War. I was unemployed for several years after the war. I finally got a job in a shoe factory but it closed in the Depression. I want to work again.

Klara Sommer: schoolteacher

> My husband died fighting for Germany in the First World War. Germany used to be a great country. Now it's weak and chaotic.

Hans Maier: factory owner

> My biggest fear is Communism. The Communists would take over my factory and close it down.

> ▼ **SOURCE 4** *A description by Albert Speer, a leading Nazi, of how he felt after hearing one of Hitler's speeches in 1931*
>
> Here it seemed to me was hope. Here were new ideals, a new understanding, new tasks. The dangers of Communism could be stopped, Hitler persuaded us, and instead of hopeless unemployment Germany could move towards economic recovery.
>
>   It must have been at this time that my mother saw a parade of stormtroopers [Hitler's private army]. The sight of such discipline in a time of chaos, and the impression of energy and hope, seems to have won her over.

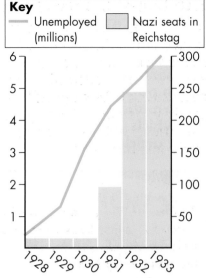

► **SOURCE 6** *A graph showing unemployment in Germany, 1928–33, and the seats the Nazi Party won in the Reichstag, 1928–33*

Key
— Unemployed (millions) ▢ Nazi seats in Reichstag

▲ **SOURCE 5** *Hitler was a powerful public speaker. This series of photos shows some of the characteristic poses he used during his speeches*

► **SOURCE 7** *An election poster for the Nazi Party, 1932. The caption reads 'Our last hope: Hitler'. The bullet list above shows some of the promises made by the Nazis in their election campaign*

The Nazis' election promises:
- create thousands of jobs
- give workers a fair deal and guarantee good wages
- protect businesses from Communism
- recover the land lost by the Treaty of Versailles
- protect our farmers from cheap foreign food
- make Germany great again.

What was life like in Nazi Germany?

The Nazis wanted to change life in Germany completely. They wanted to get everyone involved in making Germany great again . . . well, not quite everyone, as you will see! On pages 36–45 you are going to gather information about life in Nazi Germany which you will use to write a newspaper article.

▼ **DISCUSS**

1 a) What impression of life in Nazi Germany would you get if you only saw Collection A?
   b) Give Collection A a suitable title.
2 a) What impression would you get if you only saw Collection B?
   b) Give Collection B a suitable title.

COLLECTION A

▲ **SOURCE 1** *Boys in the Hitler Youth Movement singing with their friends*

▲ **SOURCE 2** *The opening of a new motorway in 1937. Motorway building projects were used by the Nazis as a way of creating jobs for the unemployed*

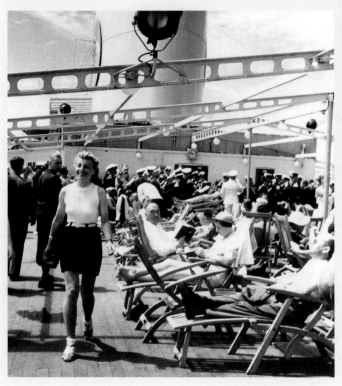

◄ **SOURCE 3** *Passengers enjoy the sun on a 'Strength Through Joy' liner, April 1939. Strength Through Joy was a Nazi organisation set up to provide affordable and wholesome leisure activities for German workers*

▼ ACTIVITY

3 Think of three questions you need to ask about each photograph to judge whether or not you can trust it to tell you the truth about Nazi Germany.

4 Why might it be misleading to base your judgement of Nazi Germany on just Collection A or just Collection B?

5 On page 45 you will write a newspaper article telling the story of Nazi Germany in either a positive or a negative way. Over pages 38–45 make notes to help you write your article.

Start by listing positive words and negative words that would be useful in your article. You can get ideas from your answers to Questions 1 and 2.

COLLECTION B

◄ SOURCE 4 *Nazi stormtroopers burn banned books in May 1933. These were books that contained ideas that did not agree with Nazi beliefs*

▲ SOURCE 5 *Political opponents of the Nazis (Communists and trade unionists) being rounded up during the election campaign of 1933. Many were then taken to concentration camps and prisons. Some were murdered*

▲ SOURCE 6 *Jewish shops in 1938 after the Nazis had told their supporters to attack Jewish properties*

WHAT WAS LIFE LIKE IN NAZI GERMANY?

Who benefited from Nazi rule?

1 The Nazis thought farmers were important to Germany, so they cancelled farmers' debts and  increased the price of farm produce so farmers had more money.

 2 The Nazis wanted strong armed forces so they recruited one million unemployed men into the army.

3 The Nazis thought women should be housewives and mothers not workers, so they sacked many female doctors, civil servants and teachers.

 4 The Nazis set up the 'Beauty of Labour' organisation to persuade employers to improve working conditions in factories. Two of its slogans were 'Good ventilation in the work place' and 'Hot meals in the factory'.

5 The Nazis put the unemployed to work on job schemes – building motorways and hospitals for example.

6 The Nazis ordered that every hen in Germany lay 65 eggs each year. If it did not, it should be slaughtered.

7 The Nazis bought a lot of vehicles, weapons and uniforms from manufacturers to equip its massive army.

8 The Nazis stopped paying unemployment benefit to anyone who refused to join a job scheme. Workers on job schemes were paid less than they had received when they were on unemployment benefit.

9 The Nazis banned big new department stores, so people would shop at small shops.

10 The Nazis made all teenage boys practise military drill in the Hitler Youth or at school, to prepare them for becoming soldiers.

11 The Nazis abolished trade unions.

12 The Nazis increased working hours in factories but kept wages low.

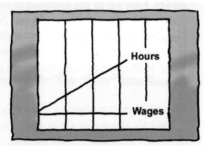

13 The Nazis gave special awards to mothers who had four or more children for service to the Fatherland.

14 The Nazis blamed the Jews for Germany's problems. They declared 600,000 Jews 'racially inferior'. They boycotted Jewish shops and closed down Jewish businesses.

15 The Nazis told manufacturers what prices they could charge. They also decided which manufacturers received the scarce raw materials.

▼ **ACTIVITY**

Statements 1–15 tell you about some of the things the Nazis did between 1933 and 1939.

1 Make a sorting frame like the one below.

Group	Positive effects	Negative effects
a) working men		
b) working women		
c) Jews		
d) the army		
e) owners of small shops		
f) manufacturers		
g) farmers		

2 Read statements 1–15. For each action by the Nazis, decide which group it affected. (Be careful: some policies affected more than one group.) Then summarise the effects by making notes in columns 2 and 3 of your sorting frame. Remember, some effects were good, some were bad. Keep your finished sorting frame safe. It will be very useful when you come to write your newspaper article (see page 45).

The causes of the Second World War

Some historians argue that the Second World War was Hitler's personal war, that he had been planning and preparing for it from before he came to power. On pages 46–55 you will examine what Hitler did to cause the Second World War, then find out if there were any other factors that led to its outbreak.

NAZI : NATIONAL SOCIAL PARTY

Hitler's war

From your earlier work you should know quite a lot about the Treaty of Versailles and about Hitler's aims and beliefs. This will be useful as you look at Hitler's foreign policy (his policy towards other countries).

I demand the reunion of Germany and Austria and the union of all German people to form a Greater Germany.

The world preaches everlasting peace, but there will never be a solution to the German problem until we return to the idea of armed struggle.

I demand the cancellation of the Treaty of Versailles, so we can rearm and regain the land taken from us by this despicable treaty.

I aimed from the start to become a destroyer of Communism. I am going to achieve this task.

The best way to use my power is in the conquest of living space [lebensraum] in the east, in Russia and Eastern Europe, and ruthlessly making everything there German.

▲ **SOURCE 1** *Hitler speaks!*

▼ ACTIVITY A

The speech bubbles in Source 1 sum up what Hitler said about his foreign policy. Copy and complete the table below. Look at Source 2 opposite to help you fill in columns 2–4.

The aims of Hitler's foreign policy	Actions he could take to achieve his aims	Who might be worried by his aims	Why they might be worried

▼ ACTIVITY B

Ask your teacher for your own copy of Source 2. Use pages 48–49 to make notes on your map about what Hitler actually did.

The Sudetenland
The richest part of Czechoslovakia, the Sudetenland, included good farming land and important raw materials and industries. Three million Germans lived in the Sudetenland. It had been part of the Austrian Empire until 1919.

The USSR
The USSR was a Communist country. Hitler hated Communism. He also regarded the Soviet people as inferior.

The Rhineland
The Treaty of Versailles banned German troops from the Rhineland in order to protect Alsace-Lorraine.

BRITAIN

EAST PRUSSIA

POLAND

USSR

N

GERMANY

CZECHOSLOVAKIA

AUSTRIA

FRANCE

0   500km

France
France had been an enemy of Germany for many years. Hitler wanted revenge for Germany's defeat in the First World War.

Austria
Hitler was Austrian. There were eight million German speakers in Austria. The Treaty of Versailles banned Austria and Germany from uniting.

The Polish Corridor
This was given to Poland in 1919 to give it access to the sea. It cut Germany in two. Many Germans lived in the Polish Corridor.

▲ **SOURCE 2** *Europe in the 1930s*

THE CAUSES OF THE SECOND WORLD WAR

What Hitler did

1935

Rearmament

As soon as Hitler came to power in 1933 he started to build up the German army and airforce. He had to do this in secret because REARMAMENT was forbidden by the Treaty of Versailles.

1936

The Rhineland

In 1936 Hitler made his first aggressive move. He ordered German soldiers to march into the Rhineland. This was forbidden by the Treaty of Versailles. Hitler justified his actions by claiming that German territory should be protected by German troops.

1938

Austria

Hitler wanted to unite Austria and Germany. This was forbidden by the Treaty of Versailles. He sent troops into Austria and forced the Austrian leader to hold a vote to see if the Austrian people wanted to join forces with Germany. He made sure the vote was rigged so that over 99 per cent of Austrians voted for unification (Anschluss).

How other countries responded

Britain and France did nothing to stop German rearmament. Many people in both countries were more worried by the power of the Communist USSR. They thought that a strong Germany might be able to protect the rest of Europe from the Communists.

No one was prepared to stop Hitler. Many thought it was reasonable for Germany to have troops in its own territory.

When the Austrian leader asked Britain, France and Italy for help, they refused. No one wanted to risk war and Hitler had promised that all he wanted now was peace.

1938

The Sudetenland

In September 1938 Hitler demanded that the Sudetenland region of Czechoslovakia join Germany. He said that most of the people who lived in this region were German and they wanted to unite with Germany.

Neville Chamberlain, the British Prime Minister, went to see Hitler three times to try to avoid war. In September 1938, Chamberlain and the French agreed that Hitler could have the Sudetenland if he promised not to take over the rest of Czechoslovakia. They did not ask the Czechs about this. This agreement is known as the 'Munich Agreement'. Chamberlain told the British people that the agreement had prevented war.

1939

Czechoslovakia

Soon afterwards, in March 1939, German troops invaded the rest of Czechoslovakia.

Britain and France did nothing to help Czechoslovakia. But it was clear that if Hitler continued his invasions then Poland would be next. Britain and France promised to help Poland if it was invaded by Hitler.

We must prepare for war. Build 1000 more aircraft.

1939

Poland

Hitler and Stalin hated each other. But in August 1939 they signed a non-aggression pact called the Nazi–Soviet Pact. They agreed not to fight each other and to divide up Poland between them. Now Hitler would not have to fight a war on two fronts. Hitler demanded back the parts of Poland that had been taken away from Germany by the Treaty of Versailles. Poland refused, and on 1 September 1939 Hitler invaded Poland.

On 3 September 1939 Britain and France declared war on Germany (although they did not send soldiers to defend Poland).

WAR

THE CAUSES OF THE SECOND WORLD WAR

▼ **ACTIVITY**

1 Sources 3–9 comment on the events that led up to the Second World War. Work out which of Hitler's actions each source refers to by using the timeline on pages 48–49.

2 Which of Sources 3–9 suggest:
   a) British leaders were weak?
   b) British leaders made mistakes?
   c) British leaders were wise and sensible?
   d) Hitler's actions were popular?
   e) Hitler took big risks?
   f) Hitler did not expect Britain to declare war?
   g) Hitler could not be trusted?
   Note: some statements could apply to more than one source.

3 Look at statements a)–g) in Question 2 again. Which do you most agree with? Write a paragraph explaining your choice.

▼ **DISCUSS**

Sources 3–7 and 9 are political cartoons.

4 Which do you think is the cleverest cartoon? Give reasons for your decision.

5 How are cartoons like these useful to historians?

6 What are the problems with using cartoons like these in history?

Primary, reliable
It shows

"Why should we take a stand about someone pushing someone else when it's all so far away .. "

INCREASING PRESSURE.

▲ **SOURCE 3** *A British cartoon from 1938. The man at the back of the row is Neville Chamberlain, the British Prime Minister*

"THERE'S SOME MISTAKE, IT WAS YOUR SMALL BROTHER I SENT FOR".

◄ **SOURCE 4**
A British cartoon from September 1939. The giant is Mars, the god of war

▲ **SOURCE 5** *A British cartoon published in 1939 showing Hitler and Stalin*

◄ **SOURCE 6** *A German cartoon published in 1938. The Austrian man on the left is saying, 'I have been longing for this since 1918'*

◄ **SOURCE 7** *A British cartoon published in 1938, featuring Neville Chamberlain, the British Prime Minister*

▼ **SOURCE 8** *Hitler speaking to his advisers in 1936*

The 48 hours after the march into the Rhineland were the most nerve-racking in my life. If the French had opposed us then we would have had to withdraw. Our forces were not strong enough even to put up a moderate resistance.

▲ **SOURCE 9** *A British cartoon published in 1936*

Why didn't the League of Nations stop Hitler?

The 1918 conference at Versailles agreed to set up a League of Nations to keep world peace. The idea was that all the countries in the world would be members and disputes would be settled by talking instead of fighting. If the countries who were arguing could not agree among themselves, then the other members of the League would force them to agree by stopping trading with them or, in the last resort, by using their armies to keep the peace. The League was eventually set up in 1919.

What was the League doing in the 1930s? The simple answer is nothing or, at least, nothing when it really mattered.

To be successful as a world peace organisation, the League of Nations needed to be supported by the world's great powers, able to act quickly and decisively and able to make countries take notice of its decisions. But the League was none of these things, as you can see from Source 10.

▼ SOURCE 10

No power

The League's only real weapon to force a country to obey its decisions was economic sanctions. But sanctions did not work because countries could still trade with non-members, particularly with the USA.

No army

The League depended on its members to supply troops. They were reluctant to risk getting involved.

Too slow

The main decision-making body, the Council, met three times a year and the Assembly only met once a year. All the decisions taken by the League had to be unanimous (everyone had to agree to them).

The weaknesses of the League of Nations

THE GAP IN THE BRIDGE.

No USA

Britain and France led the League, but the most powerful country in the world, the USA, never joined. The Americans did not want to be the world's policeman, sorting out problems in other countries. The USA therefore followed a policy known as isolationism.

The Abyssinian crisis: Mussolini gets away with it!

Mussolini, the fascist dictator in Italy, wanted an empire in Africa. In 1935 he invaded the poor country of Abyssinia (now Ethiopia).

Italy and Abyssinia were both members of the League of Nations. Abyssinia asked the League for help. The League took months to decide what to do. In the end it tried sanctions, but didn't ban the only thing that really mattered – oil – because it knew the USA would supply oil to Italy if League members did not.

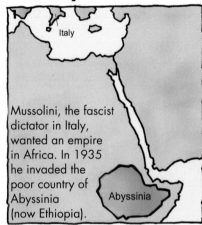

Meanwhile, Britain and France privately offered to let Mussolini have Abyssinia in return for his support against Hitler! When this news leaked out there was an uproar.

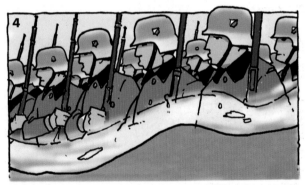

While the League was concentrating on Abyssinia, Hitler sent his troops into the Rhineland (see page 48). Abyssinia was forgotten.

While Britain and France worried about the Rhineland, Italy took Abyssinia. Mussolini had got what he wanted.

A big country had taken over a little country and the League's two leading members, Britain and France, had done little to stop it. The message to Hitler was clear. Strong countries could do as they wanted. The League was irrelevant to events in Europe.

▼ ACTIVITY

1 Read the story of the Abyssinian crisis carefully.
   a) What evidence can you find of each of the League's weaknesses outlined on page 52?
   b) What other weaknesses can you see?
2 Write a paragraph to sum up what you think is the most important reason why the League could not stand up to strong dictators.

THE CAUSES OF THE SECOND WORLD WAR

Was Appeasement a mistake?

The policy Britain and France took towards Germany in the 1930s is called Appeasement. This meant that Britain and France gave in to Hitler's demands as long as they were reasonable and prevented war. The most famous example of Appeasement was the Munich Agreement in 1938 (see page 49). Hitler was allowed to take over the Sudetenland in Czechoslovakia on the condition that he tried nothing more. When Chamberlain came back to Britain he was given a hero's welcome. He announced that the agreement promised 'peace for our time'.

▶ **SOURCE 11** *Chamberlain, the British Prime Minister, returns from the Munich Conference in Germany in 1938*

Arguments for Appeasement
Politicians at the time genuinely believed Appeasement would bring about peace. Many people in Britain in the 1930s supported the policy. And some historians today think that there were good reasons at the time to follow the policy of Appeasement as you will see on page 55.

Arguments against Appeasement
Other historians think that this policy actually helped to cause the war. They say that Hitler would not have pushed things so far if Britain and France had stood up to him earlier. Appeasement made Britain seem weak. This is a common view nowadays but some people at the time also said this.

▼ ACTIVITY

1 **Statements 1–9 on page 55 summarise the main arguments for and against Appeasement. Sort them into two groups using your own copy of the table below.**

Appeasement was the right policy	Appeasement was the wrong policy

2 **Hold a class debate on whether you think Appeasement was a reasonable policy to follow, given the circumstances.**
3 **Copy and complete the following sentences.**
   a) The policy of Appeasement may have helped to cause the war because . . .
   b) The policy of Appeasement may have been the best policy to follow because . . .

1 Germany deserved a fair deal

Many people felt that Germany had been treated unfairly by the Treaty of Versailles. They thought it was right that Germany should get back some of the land it lost in 1919. They believed that if Germany was treated fairly it would have no excuse to threaten other countries.

2 The policy of Appeasement encouraged Hitler to be more aggressive

The more he got away with, the more Hitler thought Britain and France would never put up a fight. His confidence grew until he pushed that bit too far.

3 Hitler could not be trusted

After every move, Hitler said he did not want to take over countries – but he had broken his word before.

4 We must avoid another war at all costs

People remembered the horrors of the First World War. They were determined that there should not be another war like it.

▼ **SOURCE 12** *An extract from a speech by Chamberlain to Conservative Party members in 1938*

When I think of those four terrible years [of the First World War], and I think of the seven million young men who were killed, the thirteen million who were maimed and mutilated, I felt it was my duty to strain every nerve to avoid a repetition of the First World War.

5 A powerful Germany could act as a buffer against Communism

Many politicians and people were more frightened of Communism than they were of Hitler. They were happy to let Germany get stronger so it could keep the Russian Communists at bay.

6 Appeasement made Germany too strong

Appeasement allowed Germany to grow stronger as it took over countries. From Austria it gained soldiers, gold and iron ore. From Czechoslovakia, it gained coal and weapons factories.

7 Britain's army needed time to prepare its armed forces

British generals advised Chamberlain that if war was inevitable it would be better to play for time so that more planes and weapons could be built. Britain spent a massive amount on armaments in 1938 and 1939, especially on new technology like radar and Spitfire aeroplanes.

8 Appeasement scared Stalin

When he saw that Britain would not go to war over Czechoslovakia, Stalin became convinced that Britain would not help the USSR if it were attacked. He therefore signed the Nazi–Soviet Pact with Hitler, agreeing to divide Poland instead of trying to resist German advances.

9 British people needed time

In 1938 the British people were not ready to fight a war over Czechoslovakia which they thought of as 'far away' on the other side of Europe. By 1939 British public opinion had turned in favour of going to war to stop Hitler if necessary. Countries in the British Commonwealth, like Australia and Canada, who did not support war in 1938, did so after 1939.

Review: Causes of the Second World War

▼ REVIEW ACTIVITY

CAUSE CARDS

A The Treaty of Versailles was too harsh on Germany.

B In 1939 Germany invaded Poland.

C Hitler was angry because Jesse Owens, who was black, won five gold medals at the 1936 Olympics held in Germany.

D In 1933 Hitler became Chancellor of Germany.

E Hitler wanted Germans in Austria and Czechoslovakia to be under German rule. He also wanted to take over large parts of Eastern Europe.

F France and Britain failed to stand up to Hitler early enough.

G In 1939 Portsmouth beat Wolves 4–1 in the FA Cup Final.

H The USSR and Germany signed the Nazi–Soviet Pact in 1939. It meant that Hitler would not have to fight a war on two fronts.

I The USA was not interested in what was happening in Europe.

J The world was in an economic depression between 1929 and 1933.

K Mussolini got away with invading Abyssinia.

L The League of Nations was powerless to stand up to dictators.

M In 1940 Churchill became Prime Minister of Britain.

Over pages 21–55 you have studied many different factors which helped lead to the Second World War. This task pulls the threads together, and helps you think them through. Look at cause cards A–N which show possible causes of the Second World War. Work in pairs to complete the following:

1 a) Get rid of the cause cards that you think definitely do not show a cause of the Second World War.
   b) Look at the remaining cards and think about how each one helped cause the Second World War.
   c) Write down your thoughts. You might need to refer back to pages 21–55.
2 Think about how the causes are linked. Did one cause lead directly to another?
3 Think about whether one cause is more important than another. If you took away one cause would the Second World War still have happened? If so, write a paragraph to explain your answer.
4 Think about how the causes can be classified.
   a) Group your cause cards into the following categories:
   ■ Hitler's actions
   ■ other people's actions.
   b) Think about what this tells you. Which category has the most causes? Which category contains the causes you selected as most important in Question 3?
5 Now get a sheet from your teacher to write up your conclusions.

▼ DISCUSS

6 So, do you think Hitler was totally to blame for the Second World War?

SECTION 3

THE SECOND WORLD WAR

Hitler's downfall
The Nazi state had been designed for war, but it was destroyed by war. In 1945, with his once proud army in tatters, Hitler killed himself in his air-raid shelter surrounded by the ruins of the Nazi empire.

The defeat of Germany by the Allies is one story of the Second World War, and in this section you will investigate it in detail. But there is a lot more to the Second World War than the defeat of Hitler. It was a vast conflict and there are other very important stories, which you will also study in depth:

- the story of everyday life in Britain, where all civilians took part in the war effort in one way or another
- the story of the attempted extermination of the Jewish people and other 'undesirables' in Germany, which ended in the horrors of the Holocaust
- the story of the Allied war with Japan in the Pacific and the dropping of the first nuclear bomb.

This was a harrowing period of world history that cast a long shadow over the rest of the twentieth century.

The Second World War: overview

▶▶ **On pages 60–104 you will be looking in depth at various aspects of the Second World War, but first you need to get an overview of what happened.**

The Second World War was the first truly **world** war. Most of the fighting took place in Europe, Russia, North Africa and South-East Asia, but the effects of war were felt all over the world. There were major battles on land, at sea and in the air. Civilians were affected more than in any previous war, and more civilians were killed than soldiers.

▼ DISCUSS

Here are three headings:

■ Dark days for the Allies
■ The tide turns
■ Allied victory

Where on the timeline on page 59 do you think they best fit? Write down your ideas and keep them safe. After each topic in this section, come back to these ideas and think about whether you want to change them.

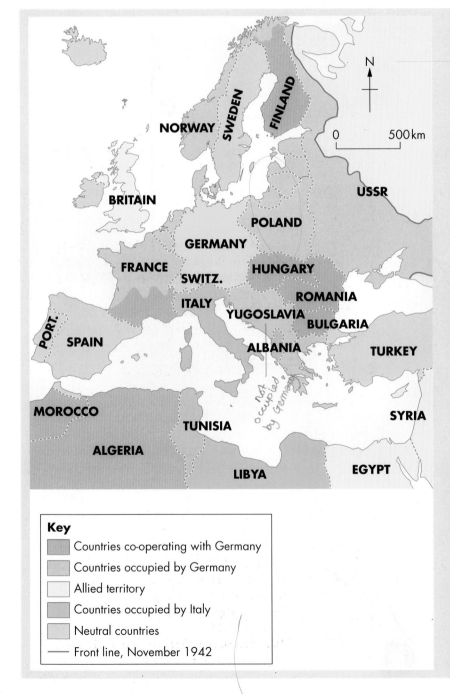

Key
- Countries co-operating with Germany
- Countries occupied by Germany
- Allied territory
- Countries occupied by Italy
- Neutral countries
- — Front line, November 1942

◀ **SOURCE 1** *A map showing Europe at the height of German domination in 1942*

The two sides

The Allies
Britain, France (although for most of the war the north was under German occupation while the south collaborated with the Nazis), the USA (from 1941), the USSR (from 1941), Australia, Canada, India and many smaller countries, particularly countries in the British Empire such as the West Indies.

The Axis powers
Germany, Japan and Italy (from 1940), supported by soldiers from a number of smaller countries such as Croatia.

WAR IN EUROPE

September 1939
Germany invades Poland. Britain declares
war on Germany.

April 1940
Germany invades Holland and France.
May 1940
The British evacuate their army from Dunkirk.
August 1940 Turning point
The Battle of Britain begins – German planes
prepare the ground for a German invasion of Britain.

Big success

February 1941
The Battle of the Atlantic begins – German U-boats
attack ships supplying Britain, cutting off supplies of
food and raw materials.
June 1941
Germany invades the USSR and advances quickly.
November 1941
The German advance in the USSR stops because
of the harsh winters.

April 1941 ~ Yugoslavia

October 1942
At the Battle of El Alamein British General Montgomery
defeats the German army and forces the
Germans out of Africa.
November 1942
The USSR begins a counter-attack against the
Germans and slowly pushes the German army back.

January 1943 Turning point
The Germany army surrenders to the USSR at
Stalingrad.
July 1943
Allied troops invade Italy.
Italy surrenders in September.

January 1944
The siege of Leningrad ends.
April 1944
The Soviet army drives the German army back to
the Russian border.
June 1944
D-Day: the Allies invade France.
August 1944
The Allies take Paris.
January 1945
The Soviet army invades Germany from the east.
February 1945
The Allies invade Germany from the west.
May 1945 V-DAY – Turning point & main event.
Germany surrenders to the Soviet army.

1939

1940

1941

1942

1943

1944

1945

WAR IN THE PACIFIC

December 1941
The Japanese attack Pearl Harbor.
The USA declares war on Japan. The Japanese
invade and occupy many Pacific islands.

June 1942
The American navy wins the Battle of Midway.
August 1942
US marines land in Guadalcanal.

January 1943
Allied gains in the Pacific continue
('island hopping').
October 1943
The Allies invade the Philippines.

February 1945
The Allies win the Philippines.
May 1945
Allied air attacks on Japan begin.
August 1945
Atomic bombs are dropped on Hiroshima and
Nagasaki. Japan surrenders.

Dunkirk: triumph or defeat?

The evacuation of British troops from Dunkirk in May 1940 is usually seen as an heroic triumph. But is this the whole story? On pages 60–63 you will examine both sides of the story, consider why interpretations of the event differ and decide whether it really was a triumph . . . or a defeat.

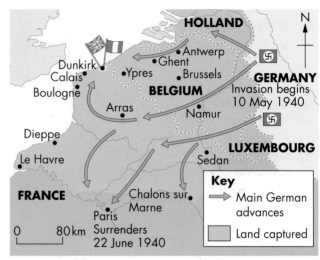

▲ **SOURCE 1** *The German advance of 1940*

The speed of the German *Blitzkrieg* (lightning war) caught the Allies by surprise. In April 1940 the German army invaded France. The German advance was so swift that the British army, and some of the French army, was pushed back to the beaches of Dunkirk. The troops were trapped between the German army and the cold waters of the English Channel. The only escape route was by sea.

There was a real danger that the entire British army (over 300,000 men) would be wiped out before the war had really got under way!

On 27 May 1940 the British government, led by Winston Churchill, put a plan called 'Operation Dynamo' into action. The aim was to evacuate the troops to Britain by ship. As well as the ships of the Royal Navy, all sorts of craft – including pleasure steamers and fishing boats – were used. Most of the soldiers were rescued.

▲ **SOURCE 2** A Daily Mirror *headline at the time*

DUNKIRK.—"TO FIGHT ANOTHER DAY"

▲ **SOURCE 5** *A cartoon published in a British newspaper at the time of the evacuation. The name of the paddle steamer is the* Brighton Belle

▼ **SOURCE 3** *A first-hand account by a gunner officer, published in 1940*

There were lines of men waiting in queues until boats arrived to transport them, a score [20] or so at a time, to the steamers and warships. The queues stood there fixed and regular, no bunching, no pushing.

▼ **SOURCE 4** *From the BBC six o'clock radio news bulletin on 31 May 1940. This was the first report about Dunkirk that was broadcast*

All night and all day men of the undefeated British Expeditionary Force have been coming home. From interviews with the men it is clear they have come back in glory; that their morale is as high as ever and that they are anxious to be back again, 'to have a real crack at Jerry [the Germans]'.

▼ **SOURCE 6** *An extract from a book published in England in July 1940*

[At Dunkirk] a miracle was born. This land of Britain is rich in heroes. She had brave daring men in her navy and air force as well as in her army. She had heroes in jerseys and sweaters and old rubber boots in all the fishing ports of Britain. That night when the word went round in all the south-east ports of Britain, there was not a man or a boy who knew how to handle a boat who was not prepared to give his own life to save some unknown son of his country who had faced, without flinching, the red hell of Flanders. For almost a week the epic went on. The little ships dodged their way up the waters and hauled over their sides the soldiers who waded waist deep to safety.

◄ **SOURCE 7** *The Withdrawal from Dunkirk, a painting by Charles Cundall, who was sent by the British government to produce an official painting of events on the beaches of Dunkirk*

▼ **ACTIVITY**

Write a newspaper article about the evacuation from Dunkirk, using Sources 1–7. This is all the information you have available. Remember, it should be a patriotic piece to help maintain British spirits. Mention:

- **the effect of the evacuation on the British and French armies**
- **what it was like on the beaches**
- **how the troops were rescued**
- **the heroism of the people who came across in the different types of boats**
- **the spirit of the rescued men.**

The end of the war in Europe

The Russian army drove the German army back. By the summer of 1944 the Germans were in full retreat. Now the Allies were prepared to invade Europe from the west. On 6 June 1944, 4000 landing craft and 600 warships carried 176,000 British, Commonwealth and North American soldiers across the English Channel. They landed at several places along the coast of Normandy, and by nightfall 120,000 men were ashore. This is known as D-Day. By the end of July there were more than a million Allied soldiers on French soil. The Germans were fighting on two fronts: mainly soldiers from Britain, the British Empire and America advancing from the west, and the Soviets from the east. It has been called 'The race to Berlin'. Both sides wanted to get there first.

By April 1945 British and American troops were within 50 miles of Berlin, and Soviet troops were in the city's eastern suburbs. On 30 April, with the sound of fighting in the background, Hitler committed suicide. On 8 May 1945 Germany surrendered.

▼ **ACTIVITY**

1 Write a sentence to explain, in your own words, why Hitler's decision to invade the USSR was a 'turning point' in the Second World War.

2 Imagine the war is over. Source 4 is to be used as a poster in Britain to thank the Soviet Union for its role in defeating Hitler. Write a headline and a short explanation to be published with the poster that explains:
   a) how the Soviets pushed the Germans back
   b) why the rest of the Allies should be grateful to the Soviets.

◀ **SOURCE 4** *A British poster intended for use in Soviet newspapers. It shows British and Soviet forces trapping Hitler*

Living through the war

▶▶ **The Second World War had a great effect on the lives of British people. For six years civilians lived dangerous and disrupted lives, as you will see in this enquiry. You will use the sources on pages 72–86 to write extracts from the diaries of people who were affected by the war.**

▼ **ACTIVITY**

On pages 72–86 you will find out a lot about life in Britain during the war. As you look at each event or development:
a) choose one of the following characters who you think might have been affected by the event or development
b) think about *how* the person might have been affected – did it change their life?
c) write a short diary extract to describe what happened to that person.

For example, after looking at Source 2 on page 72, you might write Jimmy's or Ruth's diary extract like this:

Today we got a leaflet about gas attacks. Mum made me practise putting my gas mask on and taking it off quickly. It smells horrible. She said, 'Well the smell will be worse if you don't use it. Gas will choke you to death.'

'Why would Hitler want to kill me?' I asked. Mum didn't answer, but she started to cry and ran into the kitchen.

Use your imagination but base your writing on the evidence provided.
   You'll be prompted every now and then by a task marked but don't limit yourself to those occasions. You can write about other things if you wish.

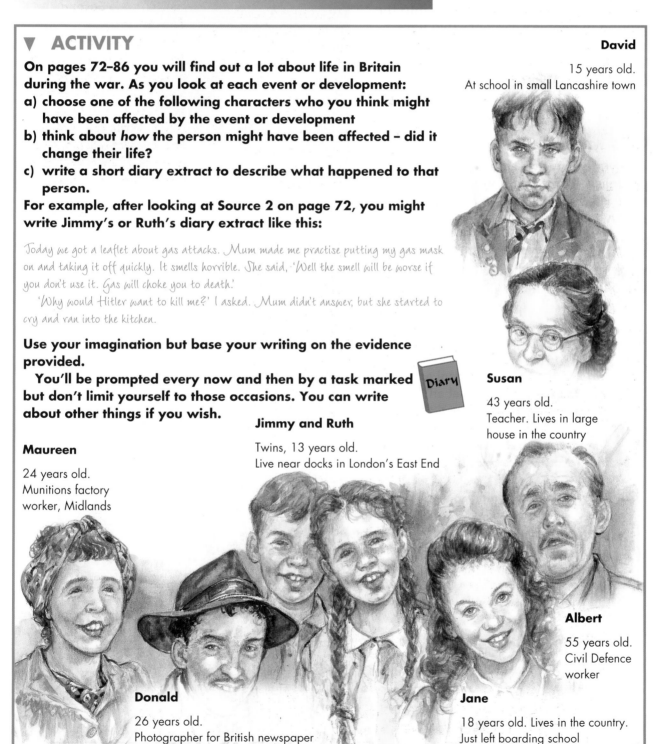

David

15 years old.
At school in small Lancashire town

Susan

43 years old.
Teacher. Lives in large house in the country

Jimmy and Ruth

Twins, 13 years old.
Live near docks in London's East End

Maureen

24 years old.
Munitions factory worker, Midlands

Albert

55 years old.
Civil Defence worker

Donald

26 years old.
Photographer for British newspaper

Jane

18 years old. Lives in the country.
Just left boarding school

LIVING THROUGH THE WAR

The journey to the country
Many of the children being evacuated were leaving home for the first time. It was very nerve-racking and frightening for some and a great adventure for others, as you can see from Sources 5–8.

► **SOURCE 5** *A boy waits to be evacuated in London's Paddington Station, May 1942*

▲ **SOURCE 6** *London schoolchildren being cared for by a member of the Women's Voluntary Service before being evacuated*

▲ **SOURCE 7** *Working-class children leaving their homes in Greater London on their way to be evacuated to the country, June 1940*

◄ **SOURCE 8** *Middle-class girls from boarding schools being evacuated, May 1940*

▼ **DISCUSS**

1 What do Sources 5 and 6 tell you about how evacuation was carried out?

2 Look at Sources 7 and 8.
   a) Are these children as worried as the children in Sources 5 and 6?
   b) Why do you think their attitude is different?

3 Photographs can be posed. Do you think any of Sources 5–8 look posed?

4 a) Which photograph do you trust most to tell you about what the children were feeling? Give reasons for your answer.
   b) How could the photograph you have chosen be misleading?

5 'Photographs are very useful to historians as evidence of how people are feeling at a particular time.' Explain why you agree or disagree with this statement.

Women at war

CONSCRIPTION was introduced in 1939. Most men aged between eighteen and 40 had to do military service. This meant that a lot of the Civil Defence work and work in factories and on the farms had to be done by women.

All single women between the ages of 19 and 30 had to register for war work. They worked in the Auxiliary Services, in the Land Army or in industry. Married women were not 'called up', because the government was worried about the effect it might have on their families, but many married women volunteered for war work anyway. Many women managed to look after their families *and* do war work.

Sources 30–37 show the wide range of work done by women during the war.

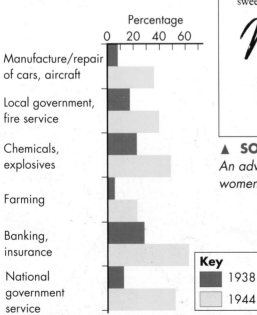

▲ **SOURCE 30** The proportion of women workers in various occupations in 1938 and 1944

Percentage
0 20 40 60

Manufacture/repair of cars, aircraft

Local government, fire service

Chemicals, explosives

Farming

Banking, insurance

National government service

Key
1938
1944

Save the situation, and the ration coupons, too, with a Mrs. Peek's Pudding! READY MADE for you by the famous house of Peek Frean, from old family recipes. Perfectly sweet, no extra sugar needed.

Mrs Peek's

PUDDING

6 *kinds: Xmas, Light Fruit, Dark Fruit, Date, Ginger, Sultana . . .*

▲ **SOURCE 31**
An advertisement in a women's magazine, 1941

▲ **SOURCE 32** A government advertisement. The Auxiliary Territorial Service was the women's branch of the army

▼ SOURCE 33 *From a speech by Clement Atlee, Deputy Prime Minister, in September 1942*

The work the women are performing in munitions [weapons] factories has to be seen to be believed. Precision engineering jobs which a few years ago would have made a skilled turner's hair stand on end are performed with dead accuracy by girls who had no industrial experience.

▼ SOURCE 35 *Forty years after the war, one woman remembers her work in the Land Army*

The people were very resentful in the country, they didn't make it easy for you, we weren't really welcome.

I was sent to a farm in Essex. There were four of us in a gang assigned to an old steam tractor with a threshing machine behind. Two of us switched the switch over and hooked the sacks on, the others threw the corn in the bin. It was very hard work. We had to go where the tackle was and sometimes we biked eight miles or so before beginning. Later I planted potatoes.

▼ SOURCE 36 *An account by a Birmingham factory worker in the early 1940s*

I'm going home to do an evening's scrubbing. First I've got to do my shopping on the way home. I have to queue for it. My two little boys are in school all day. They have their dinners there. I call for them at six o'clock. But I have to get the meal ready, and there's always some washing and mending to do every night.

◄ SOURCE 34 *Members of the Women's Land Army at work in 1942. Even before conscription to war work was introduced in 1941, 10,000 women had volunteered for it*

▼ ACTIVITY

Design a poster to be published by the government to show women all the different ways they can support the war effort.

► SOURCE 37 *Some women joined the Air Transport Auxiliary and flew newly-built planes to air bases. This photograph shows an ATA pilot who has just delivered a Wellington bomber*

Rationing

The other major change to people's lives was caused by RATIONING. This was introduced on 8 January 1940. It was needed because much of Britain's food and other goods, such as clothing, came from overseas, and German U-boats (submarines) were sinking many of the supply ships crossing the Atlantic. Most people welcomed rationing because it was fair. Before it was introduced, rich people could get whatever they wanted – if they paid enough money, but poorer people had trouble finding enough to eat.

There was also an extra allowance for luxury items such as rice, tinned fruit and cereals. Each person was given sixteen points every four weeks and could spend these points as they wished. Clothes rationing was introduced in May 1941.

Everyone had to grow as much of their own food as possible.

◀ **SOURCE 38** *A government poster showing a popular slogan, 1939*

How did the Holocaust happen?

In 1939 there were eight million Jews living in Europe. Between 1939 and 1945 six million Jewish men, women and children and other 'undesirables' were murdered in the parts of Europe controlled by the Nazis. The story of this mass murder, with the dreadful cruelty and suffering it involved, is extraordinary and disturbing. On pages 87–95 you will find out how and why it happened and prepare an IT presentation on the subject.

The background: anti-Semitism

For hundreds of years, Christian Europe had regarded the Jews as the 'Christ-killers'. At one time or another, Jews had been driven out of almost every European country. The way they were treated in England in the thirteenth century is a typical example: in 1275 all Jews were made to wear a yellow badge; 269 of them were hanged in the Tower of London in 1287.

This deep prejudice against Jews, known as anti-Semitism, was still strong in the twentieth century, especially in Germany, Poland and the Ukraine, where the Jewish population was very large. It often caused outbursts of violence, which sometimes flared up of its own accord, but sometimes was deliberately encouraged by governments. After the First World War, hundreds of Jews were murdered. In Germany, the Jews were blamed for the defeat in the war.

Prejudice against the Jews grew during the economic depression which followed. Many Germans were poor and unemployed and wanted someone to blame. They turned on the Jews, many of whom were rich and successful in business.

IMPORTANT NOTE

'Holocaust' or 'Shoah'?
This attempt to wipe out the Jewish population is usually known as the Holocaust. However, many Jews object to this term as it is associated with sacrifice. They prefer to use the word 'Shoah', which means 'whirlwind', and is used in the Old Testament to describe widespread destruction.

Not only the Jews
On pages 87–95 we will be focusing on the story of the Jews. However, hundreds of thousands of gypsies, homosexuals, Jehovah's Witnesses and mentally handicapped people, as well as four million Russian prisoners of war, were also victims of the Holocaust.

▼ ACTIVITY

1 Working in pairs, you are going to prepare a script for an IT presentation on the Holocaust. The software you will be using allows you to combine text, pictures and sound. You are preparing each screen page on paper first.

   Your presentation will be six pages long. For each page you must:

   a) write 30–40 words outlining the key information

   b) choose a photograph or an image from this section, describe what it shows and explain why you have chosen it

   c) choose a sound clip. This could be a statement from someone quoted in the sources, or it could be an interview with someone involved in the Holocaust or alive at the time, such as a Jewish survivor or a German who played no part but saw what was happening.

2 Write the first page of your presentation using the information on this page. It should introduce the topic and explain what anti-Semitism is.

How did the atomic bombs end the war in the Pacific?

▶▶ **The Second World War was really two wars – the European war and the Pacific war. On 6 August 1945, an American bomber, the *Enola Gay*, dropped the world's first atomic bomb on the Japanese city of Hiroshima. On pages 96–99 you will see how this event finally brought the Pacific war to an end.**

The background: war in the Pacific, 1941–45

The morning of Sunday 7 December 1941 was peaceful. The American Pacific Fleet was at anchor in Pearl Harbor, Hawaii. But at 7.55a.m., Japanese dive bombers swooped out of the sky and dropped bombs on every ship in the harbour and on the barracks and airfields on land. In under two hours, eighteen warships had been sunk and three damaged, 177 aircraft had been destroyed and over 2300 men had died.

The attack was a surprise. The Japanese did not declare war first. They did not warn the Americans. They hoped to destroy the entire American navy in one go, so that Japan could conquer territory throughout the Pacific without any opposition from the USA.

Although the Japanese did not destroy the entire American navy, they did harm it. In the months after the attack on Pearl Harbor, the Japanese conquered a lot of land (see Source 1).

From 1942 onwards Allied troops fought to regain this land, mile by mile, island by island. It was a bitter war, fought in terrible conditions. Allied prisoners of war were treated particularly brutally by the Japanese.

As the Allies got nearer to Japan, the Japanese used KAMIKAZE pilots and suicide squads on the ground to fight every step of the Allied advance. The Japanese soldiers were told not to surrender. The only way for the Allies to take an island was for them to kill or capture all the soldiers. At Iwo Jima, 22,400 out of the 23,000 Japanese defenders were killed.

Key
- ▮ Land held by Japan, December 1941
- ▮ Land captured by Japan, July 1942

▲ **SOURCE 1** *A map of the area involved in the war in the Pacific*

▲ **SOURCE 2** *Ships ablaze after the attack on Pearl Harbor, 1941*

SOURCE 3 *In 1942 the Japanese planned to invade India. To help transport their troops they built a railway linking Thailand and South Burma. The railway was 415 km long and passed through the most appalling terrain. It was built by prisoners of war. This account of the life of prisoners working on the railway was written in 1988 and is based on interviews with some of the prisoners*

During the monsoons [rain storms] the men struggled back to their huts and often found them awash with human excrement. The sick suffered terribly. The Japanese cry of 'No work – No food' brought a shudder to those poor souls suffering from dysentery, malaria and tropical ulcers. The ravages of cholera were especially horrific.

Many of the jungle camps were of huts made of bamboo. They leaked. The dampness and the humidity of the jungle rotted clothes and encouraged vast swarms of malaria-carrying mosquitoes. Some men became blind through lack of vitamins. The prisoners often started sixteen hours of work with only a cupful of cold rice and a mug of cold tea with no sugar or milk to give them nourishment.

SOURCE 5 *An extract from* The Road to Mandalay, *written in 1961 by J. Masters*

The Japanese are the bravest people I have ever met. In attack they simply came on, using all their skill and rage, until they were stopped by death. In defence they held their ground with furious determination. They had to be killed company by company, squad by squad, man by man to the last.

SOURCE 6 *A first-hand account of battles between British and Japanese soldiers around Rangoon in Burma in 1942*

One tank was knocked out by a Jap mortar. The Japs were nowhere to be seen, yet the tanks were fired on from all directions. When the crews bailed out the Japanese were waiting for them with bayonets.

There were scores of Japs killed and many snipers hung dead in the palm tree tops where they had tied themselves. The Japs used snipers a lot. They were camouflaged and almost invisible. In the heavy forest they were difficult to detect. The snipers worked in pairs, one man to distract the enemy while his colleague was able to shoot undetected. Japanese infiltration parties would creep up to the tanks and lob in hand-grenades.

▲ **SOURCE 4** *British prisoners of war in the medical section of a Japanese prisoner-of-war camp*

▼ ACTIVITY

1 **Using Sources 3–6, describe the hardships and dangers faced by Allied soldiers fighting the Japanese.**
2 **What do you think the Americans and the Japanese might have been feeling as they faced the prospect of an Allied invasion of Japan?**
   a) **Choose three words to describe the feelings of the Americans.**
   b) **Choose three words to describe the feelings of the Japanese.**

The event: the bombing of Hiroshima and Nagasaki, August 1945

For some years, American scientists had been working on a totally new type of bomb – the atomic bomb. In March 1945 they carried out their first successful test. They could not predict the full effects of the bomb, but they knew it was powerful. They had only two more bombs, but each had the power to destroy a city.

The scientists informed the President of the USA that the bombs were ready to use. You can probably guess the feelings of the American leaders as they heard the news. The USA believed that the Japanese would never surrender. Japan had 5000 aircraft, and five million soldiers prepared to fight to the death. Hundreds of thousands more American soldiers could be killed if attacks on the islands of Japan continued. President Harry Truman had no hesitation at all in approving the use of the bomb, because it would save so many American lives.

On 6 August 1945 the bomber, *Enola Gay*, dropped the first atomic bomb on Hiroshima. There was a glaring pinkish light in the sky, which burned out people's eyes. Anyone within a kilometre of the explosion became a bundle of smoking black charcoal within seconds. Within minutes about 70,000 people were dead. Those who were still alive writhed in agony from their burns. Then there was the blast wave, which destroyed 70,000 of the city's 78,000 buildings. Sources 8–12 show the impact of the bomb on Hiroshima.

The Americans asked the Japanese to surrender. The Japanese refused. Three days later the Americans dropped a second atomic bomb on Nagasaki killing 36,000 people. Six days later Japan surrendered. The war in the Pacific was over.

▼ **SOURCE 7** *An extract from* The Road to Mandalay, *written in 1961 by J. Masters*

By the summer of 1945, the Americans were ready to invade Japan itself. US experts thought their invasion could succeed but that Allied casualties would be massive as the Japanese fought to defend their own home territory. Experts reported that the Japanese had strengthened their defences. The Allies called on Japan to surrender but its military government refused. It seemed that they would fight to the last man.

► **SOURCE 8** *Hiroshima after the blast*

▼ **SOURCE 9** *An extract from J. Hersey's account of the effects of the bomb, published in 1946*

Father Kleinsorge found about twenty men in the bushes. They were all in the same nightmarish state; their faces were wholly burned, their eye sockets hollow, the fluid from their melted eyes had run down their cheeks. Their mouths were mere swollen, pus-covered wounds, which they could not bear to stretch enough to admit the spout of a teapot. So Father Kleinsorge got a large piece of grass and drew out the stem so as to make a straw and give them all the water to drink that way.

Source 8 Description }
- Isolated
- Silence
- No living-Beings
- demolished
- destroyed
- devastation
- ruined
- destruction
- blast

▼ **SOURCE 10** *An eyewitness account by a girl who was five years old at the time*

The skin was burned off some of them and was hanging from their hands and from their chins.

▼ **SOURCE 11** *A Japanese eyewitness account of radiation sickness*

Survivors began to notice in themselves a strange form of illness. It consisted of vomiting, loss of appetite, diarrhoea with large amounts of blood, purple spots on the skin, bleeding from the mouth, loss of hair and usually death.

▼ **SOURCE 12** *Three weeks after the bomb a British journalist, W. Burchett, managed to get to Hiroshima. He wrote the first public account of radiation sickness. It appeared in an article in the Daily Express*

I write this as a warning to the world. In Hiroshima, 30 days later, people who were not injured in the bombing are still dying mysteriously and horribly from an unknown something which I can only describe as the atomic plague.

▼ **ACTIVITY**

1 Read Source 7. Choose three words to describe President Truman's feelings when he heard that the bomb was ready and could be used as a weapon.
2 Study Source 9. What else do you think eyewitnesses would have seen as they walked around Hiroshima? Using Sources 8–12 to help you, write several sentences or paragraphs to add to J. Hersey's account.

▼ **DISCUSS**

3 Read Source 12. The Americans banned journalists from reporting from Hiroshima. At first, they also denied the existence of radiation sickness. Why do you think they did this?

What was the Cold War?

After the end of the Second World War a different sort of war began – a cold war. In this enquiry you will find out what this involved and why it was so dangerous.

During the Second World War the USA and the USSR fought on the same side against Nazi Germany. But at the end of the war they fell out. This was because the USA was a CAPITALIST country and the USSR was a Communist country. They had different ways of life and they both thought their way of doing things was the right way.

The Communists take over Eastern Europe
After the war the USSR took control of a large part of Eastern Europe and helped Eastern European countries to set up Communist governments. The Russian leader, Stalin, said he wanted to have friendly countries between the Soviet Union and the West to act as a buffer against invasion. By 1949 Europe was divided between the Communist countries in the east and the democratic countries in the west. The dividing line became known as the 'iron curtain'.

An iron curtain has descended across Europe. Behind that line all the countries and peoples of Central and Eastern Europe lie under Soviet control.

▲ **SOURCE 1** *Winston Churchill, March 1946*

Capitalist USA	Communist USSR
• Hold elections to choose government	• One party dictatorship
• Business owned privately and driven by desire to make profits	• Industries and farms owned and run by the state
• Property owned privately	• No individual ownership of property
• Individual freedom very important	• Individuals' lives tightly controlled

The Americans help Western Europe
The USA and other western democratic countries like Britain and France believed that the USSR wanted to take over the whole of Europe. The Americans sent millions of dollars, which they called Marshall Aid, to countries in Western Europe to help them rebuild after the war. These countries started to become more prosperous while the Communist East remained poor. The Soviet Union said the USA was using its great wealth to bribe or force other countries to follow the American way of life.

The Communist countries put up high fences with guard towers along their borders so nobody could get in or out.

▲ **SOURCE 2** *Divisions between Eastern and Western Europe, 1949*

► **SOURCE 3**

Why do you want to strengthen your currency? Why don't you try mine?

Is it difficult to carry out your policy? Carry out ours!

The arms race

The USA and the USSR both built nuclear weapons to threaten each other.

They improved the ways of delivering the bombs. The first bombs at Hiroshima and Nagasaki were dropped from an aeroplane but, soon, both sides had developed missiles that could be fired thousands of miles by rockets. By the 1960s each side had so many bombs that the world would be destroyed many times over if they were ever launched.

Britain was on the USA's side. American missiles were stationed in Britain and any Soviet attack on the USA would include attacks on Britain's major cities.

Some said that nuclear bombs made the world **safer**. Neither side dared to use them because they knew that if they struck first, the other side would retaliate, thereby destroying both countries.

Others said the nuclear bombs made the world **more dangerous** because one mistake could start an attack that would kill most of the people in both countries, as well as many others, as the radiation spread around the globe.

From launch to detonation takes around 30 minutes.

Long-range missiles were based in the USA and the USSR.

USSR

USA

Short-range missiles were based in Western Europe.

▲ **SOURCE 4** *American and Soviet missile locations. Long-range missiles would take 30 minutes to arrive. Short-range missiles from Western Europe could hit the USSR in a few minutes*

▼ DISCUSS

1 Look at the cartoons in Source 3. Do they show
   a) the American view of Soviet foreign policy
   or
   b) the Soviet view of American foreign policy?
   Explain how you came to your decision.

▼ ACTIVITY

2 Why do you think Churchill called the line dividing Europe the Iron Curtain?

3 Write a paragraph to explain how Europe got divided in this way.

WHAT WAS THE COLD WAR?

What happened in the Cold War?

Although the USA and the Soviet Union were enemies and deeply distrusted each other, they never fought each other directly. A 'hot war' never developed – maybe because the risk of nuclear war made everyone cautious. Instead, from the 1940s to the 1980s, the two superpowers entered into a 'cold war'. They:

- threatened and spied on each other
- put out negative propaganda against each other
- poured masses of money into weapons and bombs
- sent money, weapons or soldiers to other countries to fight wars.

Sometimes the relationship between the two sides improved, sometimes it got worse.

▼ ACTIVITY

1. **What do you think are the main differences between a capitalist way of life and a communist way of life? (Look at pages 106–109.)**
2. **Why do you think the USA and the USSR never actually fought each other?**
3. **What effects do you think the Cold War had in the places where it was fought like Vietnam, Afghanistan and Africa?**
4. **Work in groups, using the Internet or CD-ROMS like Encarta, to find out about the hot spots in the Cold War. Each group should choose a hot spot and present their findings back to the class.**

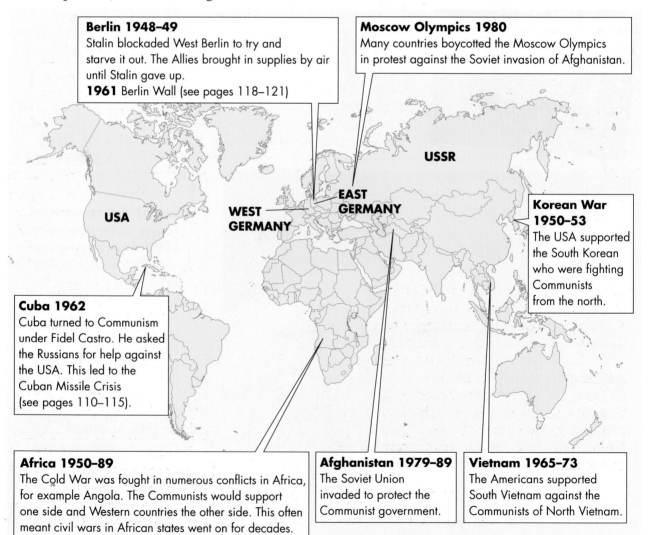

Berlin 1948–49
Stalin blockaded West Berlin to try and starve it out. The Allies brought in supplies by air until Stalin gave up.
1961 Berlin Wall (see pages 118–121)

Moscow Olympics 1980
Many countries boycotted the Moscow Olympics in protest against the Soviet invasion of Afghanistan.

Korean War 1950–53
The USA supported the South Korean who were fighting Communists from the north.

Cuba 1962
Cuba turned to Communism under Fidel Castro. He asked the Russians for help against the USA. This led to the Cuban Missile Crisis (see pages 110–115).

Africa 1950–89
The Cold War was fought in numerous conflicts in Africa, for example Angola. The Communists would support one side and Western countries the other side. This often meant civil wars in African states went on for decades.

Afghanistan 1979–89
The Soviet Union invaded to protect the Communist government.

Vietnam 1965–73
The Americans supported South Vietnam against the Communists of North Vietnam.

USA   WEST GERMANY   EAST GERMANY   USSR

▲ **SOURCE 5** *Hot spots in the Cold War*

The American policy towards the Soviet Union during the Cold War was called 'Containing Communism'. The Americans supplied soldiers, weapons and money to countries fighting Communism.

For example, from 1965 to 1973 the USA provided soldiers and weapons to support the South Vietnamese government which was fighting the Communists in North Vietnam. The Americans pulled out of Vietnam when it became clear they could not win. Vietnam became Communist. Containment policy had failed.

The Soviet Union supported Communists in other countries by supplying them with money and weapons. Sometimes they got more directly involved. For example, in 1979 the Soviet army invaded neighbouring Afghanistan to make sure that a Communist government stayed in power. The USA sent weapons to help the Afghan rebels. After ten years of war, the Soviet Union and the Communist government of Afghanistan were defeated.

Communism is an evil virus that is spreading across the world. We must stop the disease from spreading.

In Communist countries, people are enslaved and have no freedom to say or do what they want. They are not even allowed to leave their countries.

The Russians are planning world conquest. They want to pull other countries into their 'evil empire'.

Countries in the world should live the American Way which brings freedom wealth and happiness.

Force is the only thing the Russians understand. The United States is the only country strong enough to resist them.

Capitalist countries are trying to surround us and destroy our way of life.

If the capitalist way of life is so good, why are there so many poor people in the USA?

In the Soviet Union everybody is guaranteed a job, a wage and a place to live.

Americans control the world's trade and world prices so that poorer countries never get a chance to get a fair price for their products. America stays rich by keeping other countries poor.

The American way of life is sick – it is all about goods and things people have. It makes people selfish and greedy.

What happened next?

Kennedy ignored the advice to invade. He accepted Khrushchev's offer. On 28 October Khrushchev and Kennedy came to an agreement. The crisis was over! The missile sites were dismantled and the missiles returned to the USSR while observers from the United Nations watched.

Kennedy

Khrushchev

Kennedy came out of the crisis smiling. Some historians think that Kennedy saved the world from nuclear war. They believe that the blockade put pressure on the Soviets, without causing a war. The strong threats Kennedy used made the Russians remove the missiles, but he gave them enough time to think and a way to save face.

Khrushchev also came out of the crisis smiling. Other historians think that it was Khrushchev, not Kennedy, who saved the world from nuclear war. On the brink of war, he pulled back. When he saw that Kennedy could not be pushed around, he was not prepared to risk causing a nuclear war. He showed that he was not too proud or stupid to put a stop to such a dangerous plan.

Some say the world was safer as a result of the Cuban Missile Crisis. Both the Americans and the Soviets realised how close they had come to blowing up the world. To reduce the danger of this ever happening again they:

- set up a telephone link between Washington and Moscow, so the countries could contact each other in seconds. This could be very important if there were only a few minutes to decide whether or not to launch a nuclear strike
- agreed to ban nuclear testing above ground.

However, relations between the two superpowers remained very cool for the next thirty years as you have seen on pages 108–109.

▼ ACTIVITY

You are going to write a newspaper article about the Cuban Missile Crisis. It could be:
a) a balanced account of the events
b) an account biased in favour of Kennedy
c) an account biased in favour of Khrushchev.

You could use one of the following headlines:

Courageous Kennedy safeguards world peace!

Kennedy brings the world to the brink of nuclear disaster!

In your article you should mention:

- how the crisis began (you can get ideas from your answer to Question 1 on page 111)
- the choices Kennedy faced (you can get ideas from your answer to Question 2 on page 111)
- the events of October 1962 (see pages 112–114)
- how much of a threat the crisis was to world peace (you can get ideas from your crisis graph on page 113).

Can you think like a Cold War leader?

▶▶ **The Cold War was a battle of propaganda and threats. The leaders of the USA and the USSR had to stay one step ahead of each other, without causing a war. Can you do the same?**

▼ ACTIVITY

Play this game to see if you can think like a Cold War leader.

1 **Work in pairs or small groups. Decide whether you are going to be the leader of the USA or the leader of the USSR. It does not matter which you choose.**

2 **You have a series of decisions to make. For each decision, choose which of the three options you think will help you stay one step ahead of your enemy in the Cold War.**

3 **Each option is worth ten, five or zero points. You need to work out which you think is worth more. Sometimes two options will be worth the same number of points so think hard about each decision.**

4 **Your teacher will tell you your score after you have made each decision. This gives you time to think about any mistakes you might have made before you move on to the next decision. By the time you get to round nine, you should really be thinking like a Cold War leader.**

START

Application for Residency

Round one

One of your enemy's most famous celebrities asks to come to live in your country because he likes it better than his own. Do you:
a) appear on television giving him a medal for doing such a brave thing
b) order the request to be kept secret, but call him to your office for a secret meeting
c) refuse permission, ignore him and get on with more important things like fighting poverty in your own country?

Round eight

One of your oil tankers has been wrecked and a massive oil slick is floating towards your enemy's coastline. Do you:
a) offer to send all the help your enemy needs to clean the mess up
b) do nothing – it's your enemy's problem
c) accuse your enemy of deliberately luring the tanker onto the rocks?

Round seven

Your opposite number makes a speech saying your government is a danger to world peace.
Do you:
a) make a speech saying the same thing about him
b) leak a story to the newspapers, claiming that he is going mad or that he is desperate because he is losing support in his own country
c) admit your failings to your country in a live television broadcast and promise to try harder in future?

Round two

Your spies tell you that your enemy has made a new bomb. Do you:

a) order your spies to find out more so you can copy the bomb

b) send soldiers to destroy the bomb

c) phone your enemy to check if what your spies have told you is correct and to suggest that they should be more careful?

Round three

An African country asks for your help to fight its neighbour, who supports your enemy in the Cold War. Do you:

a) send trained peace negotiators to try to prevent fighting

b) offer to sell them as many weapons as they need at knock-down prices

c) send your best soldiers to train their army?

Round nine

Your enemy has launched a rocket into space. Do you:

a) tell your scientists to do the same

b) shoot your enemy's rocket down

c) offer to collaborate with your enemy to develop a peaceful space programme?

FINISH

Round four

The President of the enemy country invites you to a secret, off-the-record summit meeting so the two of you can try to understand each other better. Do you:

a) refuse to have anything to do with such a dangerous person

b) agree to the meeting, as long as he promises to treat the people in his country better

c) agree to the meeting and suggest a game of golf and a vodka afterwards?

Round six

One of your enemy's submarines is in trouble near your coastline. Do you:

a) rescue the sailors in a blaze of publicity and return them to their country in your private plane

b) accuse your enemy of trying to start a war and give them two days to get the submarine out of your waters

c) secretly send your own navy to sink the submarine?

Round five

Your enemy wins more gold medals at the Olympic Games than your country does. Do you:

a) accuse your enemy of cheating, of using drugs and special training programmes

b) secretly find out your enemy's training methods and insist your athletes use them

c) boycott the next Olympic Games in protest at something your enemy has done?

What was so important about the Berlin Wall?

▶▶ **The Berlin Wall separated Communist East Berlin from Capitalist West Berlin for thirty years. It became a symbol of the distrust and tension caused by the Cold War. On pages 118–121 you will study the story of the Berlin Wall.**

1945–61: Before the Wall

1

After the war Germany was divided. Communist East Germany was run by the Soviet Union and democratic West Germany was run by Britain, the USA and France.

2

Berlin, the capital of Germany, was also divided into Communist East Berlin and democratic West Berlin.

3

From the outset, the USA and the Soviet Union argued over Berlin. Both sides filled Berlin with spies and soldiers.

4

The USA and its allies poured money into West Germany. They tried to make West Berlin a good advert for democracy and capitalism: workers in the city earned good wages and had an excellent standard of living.

5 Communist East Germany did not do so well. Workers were guaranteed jobs, but they were poorly paid and there were constant shortages of everyday goods. The Communist government controlled every aspect of East Germans' lives.

6 Many East Germans fled to West Germany believing their lives would be better there. This was embarrassing for the Communists. It was also damaging for East Germany because those who left were among East Germany's most skilled citizens.

1961–85: Living with the wall

On 13 August 1961 the Communists built a wall along the border between East and West Berlin and from this point on, refused to let anyone leave East Berlin without a permit. It was almost impossible to get a permit. The wall cut through the middle of communities. Some families woke up to find that they could no longer visit relatives on the other side of the city.

East German border guards were ordered to shoot dead anyone trying to cross the wall. Only one week after the wall was erected Rudolf Urban was the first to die when he tried to escape by jumping from a window.

In 1962, Peter Fechter was shot by border guards as he tried to climb the wall. The guards left him to bleed to death under their checkpoint.

Some did manage to escape. In 1965, one of the most daring escapes took place. The Holzapfel family slid across the wall on an aerial runway with the help of friends from West Berlin. More than 200 people died trying to escape to West Berlin. More than 5000 successfully escaped, by boat, balloon, tunnel and lorry. This figure includes 500 border guards who also decided they had had enough of East Germany.

The Berlin Wall became the symbol of the Cold War. Only a few hundred yards of concrete and barbed wire separated the two worlds of capitalism and Communism.

1985–90: The wall comes down

TIME PASSED

TWENTY YEARS LATER

The Berlin Wall might have stopped people escaping, but it could **not** stop East Germans getting fed up with Communism. If they protested, however, the army sent in tanks to keep them quiet.

In 1985, Mikhail Gorbachev became the new leader of the Soviet Union. Gorbachev wanted the USSR to change, to become more open and free. He wanted other Communist countries to change too.

In East Germany, thousands of protesters came out on the streets agreeing with him. The East German leader asked Gorbachev to send tanks to stop the protests and to restore order. Gorbachev told him that East Germany was now on its own.

In 1989, thousands of East Germans marched to the Berlin Wall.

The border guards threw down their rifles and joined the protesters. In November 1989 thousands of East Berliners and West Berliners dismantled the wall with hammers and chisels.

▲ SOURCE 1

The demolition of the Berlin Wall was one of the most powerful events in Cold War history. The wall was a symbol of distrust and division, and it was removed by ordinary people from both sides. For many people, it marked the end of the Cold War.

East Germans and West Germans celebrated as their country was reunited. In the months that followed, other Communist countries also elected non-Communist governments. In 1991 the Soviet Union itself disintegrated into fifteen separate republics, each with a non-Communist government. The Cold War was over.

▼ **ACTIVITY**

Source 1 is to be used in an exhibition about the Cold War. Write a caption to be displayed alongside the picture. The caption should explain why the collapse of the Berlin Wall was such a significant event. You will need to explain:

a) **what the Cold War was**

b) **how the wall became a symbol of the Cold War**

c) **why it was pulled down**

d) **why its demolition was such a significant event.**

▼ ACTIVITY

Gandhi is most famous for his campaign for Indian independence, but he had many other ideas as well. Here are some of the other things he said:

Toleration is the only thing that will enable people of different religions to live as good neighbours and friends.

The world of tomorrow will be, **must be**, a society based on non-violence. Out of this all other blessings will flow. An individual can adopt the way of life of the future – the non-violent way – without having to wait for others to do so. And if the individual can do it, cannot whole groups of individuals? Cannot whole nations?

In a plan of life based on non-violence, woman has as much right to shape her own destiny as man has to shape his.

In true democracy, every man and woman is taught to think for himself or herself.

Let there be no distinction between rich and poor, high or low.

History is a record of perpetual wars, but we are now trying to make new history.

The whole world is like the human body with its various parts. Pain in one part is felt in the whole body.

How relevant are Gandhi's ideas in the twenty-first century? You are going to prepare for a debate on this topic.

1 **Research newspaper articles and pictures that you think show situations in which Gandhi's ideas (see above) are shown to be true or false. Try to find one story that relates to each of the quotations.**

2 **Use your newspaper articles and pictures to help you prepare a speech either for or against the motion: 'Gandhi's ideas are irrelevant in the context of the modern world'.**
Your teacher can give you a sheet to help you write your speech.

Review: The Twentieth Century World

▼ **REVIEW ACTIVITY**

In this book you have studied some of the major topics of twentieth century history. It has not told the whole story of the twentieth century. It has concentrated on a selection of key people and events.

Gandhi

Hitler   the Holocaust

Stalin

the atomic bomb   the Cold War

Churchill

the Cuban Missile Crisis

the trenches

We have interpreted twentieth century history by covering the parts that we think are important. You are now going to create your own interpretation of the twentieth century.

1 From all that you know about the twentieth century, either from this book or from your own knowledge, choose:
   a) one event, *and*
   b) one person
   that you think was particularly important and
   deserves to be remembered.
2 Think about how this event or person made life better for people, or made life worse, and why the event or person deserves to be remembered.
3 Write a paragraph explaining your choice.
4 Record your ideas about the lessons you would like the world to learn from the history of the twentieth century. You could use this writing frame as a starting point.

In my opinion the lessons we should learn from the twentieth century are:

_____

_____

The most important one is

_____

because

_____

Glossary

ALLIANCES   an agreement between two or more countries to support each other

ARMISTICE   a truce, when both sides agree to stop fighting for a time

ARTILLERY   heavy guns. The Royal Artillery is the part of the army that uses them

BANKRUPT   having no money

CAPITALIST   people who believe in an economic system in which the production and distribution of goods depend on private money and profit making

COLONIES   a country which is run by the government of another country

COMMUNIST   a person or political party that seeks a society in which all property is publicly owned and each person is paid and works according to his or her needs and abilities

COMPANY   see REGIMENT

COMPENSATION   money given by Germany to pay for the damage and loss of life caused by the war

CONSCRIPTION   a law that forces all men (and sometimes women) to join the armed forces if and when they are needed

CO-OPERATIVE   a farm or business owned and run jointly by its members. All profits and benefits are shared out among them equally

DEPRESSION   a long period of financial and industrial decline

DRESSING STATIONS   a place for giving emergency treatment to the wounded

DUGOUT   a roofed shelter built into the wall of a trench

EMPIRE   a group of countries, or COLONIES, that are under the authority of the country which conquered them

EVACUATE   to move people out of a dangerous area

FASCIST   a person or political party with extreme right-wing views, often including racism, nationalism and complete obedience to authority

FRONT LINE   the land nearest the enemy, where the fighting takes place

GHETTO   an enclosed part of a city where Jews had to live

KAMIKAZI   a pilot who deliberately crashes his aircraft on its target

NEUTRAL   a country is neutral if it does not side with countries involved in a conflict

PALS REGIMENT   see REGIMENT

RADAR   a system for detecting the presence and position of aircraft and ships etc.

RATIONING   giving every person an officially fixed amount of certain sorts of food, fuel or clothing, when they are in short supply

REARMAMENT   building up a new store of weapons, or replacing old weapons with better ones

REGIMENT   a unit of an army usually commanded by a colonel and divided into several COMPANIES. PALS units were made up of people from the same town or area

REPARATIONS   compensation for war damage paid by the defeated country

REPUBLIC   a country in which supreme power is held by the elected representative of the people, not by a monarch

SABOTAGE   deliberate damage of equipment or resources in order to hinder progress

SOVIET   belonging to the USSR (the Union of Soviet Socialist Republics), which is also known as the Soviet Union

SS   Schutzstaffel, the Nazi secret police force

STALEMATE   a situation in which no progress can be made

STOCK MARKET   where company stocks and shares are bought and sold

UNITED NATIONS   an international peace-keeping organisation

VICEROY   a ruler exercising authority on behalf of a monarch in a COLONY

Index

INDEX

Acknowledgements

Thanks are due to the following for permission to reproduce copyright photographs:

Cover Imperial War Museum, London; **p.v** *t* Imperial War Museum, London, *tm* AKG London, *bm* Imperial War Museum, London, *b* Leslie Illingworth, Centre for the Study of Cartoons and Caricature, University of Kent, Canterbury; **p.vi** *tl* Imperial War Museum, London, *tr* AKG London, *b* Imperial War Museum, London; **p.1** *tl* Popperfoto, *tr* Popperfoto, *bl* The Art Archive, *br* AKG London; **p.2** *tr* Imperial War Museum, London, *tm* AKG London, *bml* Hulton Archives, *bmc* Hulton Archives, *bmr* The Art Archive, *b* AKG London; **p.3** *t* Mary Evans Picture Library, *b* Imperial War Museum, London; **p.5** Imperial War Museum, London; **p.11** Peter Newark's Military Pictures; **p.12** Imperial War Museum, London; **p.13** *t* Imperial War Museum, London, *b* The Illustrated London News Picture Library; **p.17** IWM 30174(1656) Over the Top, 1st Artists' Rifles at Marcoing, 30th December 1917 by John Northcote Nash (1893–1977) Imperial War Museum, London, UK/Bridgeman Art Library. With permission from the John Nash Estate; **p.18** The Art Archive/ Imperial War Museum; **p.19** Imperial War Museum, London; **p.21** *tl* Mary Evans Picture Library, *tr* Mary Evans/Explorer Archives, *b* Mary Evans Picture Library; **p.25** *t* Mary Evans Picture Library, *b* Simplicissimus; **p.27** *t* Mary Evans Picture Library, *m* Mary Evans Picture Library, *b* Mary Evans/Explorer Archives; **p.30** David King Collection; **p.31** David King Collection; **p.32** *t* AKG London, *b* © Bildarchiv Preußischer Kulturbesitz (bpk), Berlin; **p.35** *l* Mary Evans Picture Library, *r* AKG London; **p.36** *tl* Süddeutscher Verlag Bilderdienst, *tr* Ullstein Bilderdienst, *b* Ullstein Bilderdienst; **p.37** *t* Imperial War Museum, London, *bl* Bundesarchiv, Bild 102/2920, *br* © Bildarchiv Preußischer Kulturbesitz (bpk), Berlin; **p.41** *both* AKG London; **p.44** Mary Evans Picture Library; **p.45** *b* Mary Evans Picture Library; **p.46** Mary Evans Picture Library; **p.50** *t* David Low, The *Evening Standard*, Centre for the Study of Cartoons and Caricature, University of Kent, Canterbury, *m* The *Daily Express*, *b* David Low, The *Evening Standard*, Centre for the Study of Cartoons and Caricature, University of Kent, Canterbury; **p.51** *t* *Simplicissimus*, *m* *News of the World*, *b* David Low, The *Evening Standard*, Centre for the Study of Cartoons and Caricature, University of Kent, Canterbury; **p.52** *b* © Punch Ltd; **p.54** Hulton Archives; **p.60** Imperial War Museum, London; **p.61** David Low, The *Evening Standard*, Centre for the Study of Cartoons and Caricature, University of Kent, Canterbury; **p.62** Imperial War Museum, London; **pp.64–65** Topham Picturepoint; **p.67** Imperial War Museum; **p.69** David Low, The *Evening Standard*, Centre for the Study of Cartoons and Caricature, University of Kent, Canterbury; **p.70** Public Record Office Image Library INF2/31; **p.72** *t* Topham Picturepoint, *b* Imperial War Museum, London; **p.74** *both* Hulton Archives; **p.75** *both* Hulton Archives; **p.77** Imperial War Museum, London; **p.78** Topham Picturepoint; **p.79** Popperfoto; **p.80** Sidney 'George' Strube, The *Daily Express*, The Centre for the Study of Cartoons and Caricature, University of Kent, Canterbury; **p.82** *t* Hulton Archives, *m* Popperfoto, *b* Hulton Archives; **p.83** © Noreen Branson; **p.84** *t* Mary Evans Picture Library, *b* Public Record Office Image Library INF3/119; **p.85** *t* Popperfoto, *b* The Art Archive; **p.86** Imperial War Museum, London; **p.88** *t* Weiner Library, *b* Imperial War Museum, London; **p.89** *t* By permission of Mr J. Spears, *b* Mary Evans Picture Library; **p.90** AKG, London; **p.91** © Yad Vashem Photo Archive; **p.92** Hulton Archives; **p.93** *t* Weiner Library, *b* Popperfoto; **p.94** © Yad Vashem Photo Archive; **p.96** Popperfoto; **p.97** Camera Press London; **pp.98–99** The Art Archive; **p.101** Victor Weisz 'Vicky', The *Evening Standard*, Centre for the Study of Cartoons and Caricature, University of Kent, Canterbury; **p.105** Leslie Illingworth, The *Daily Mail*, Centre for the Study of Cartoons and Caricature, University of Kent, Canterbury; **p.107** *r and l* School of Slavonic and East European Studies, University of London; **p.110** Popperfoto; **p.114** *l* Rex Features Limited, *r* AKG, London; **p.121** AKG London; **p.124** Popperfoto.

t = top, *b* = bottom, *m* = middle, *l* = left, *r* = right

Every effort has been made to trace all copyright holders, but if any have been inadvertently overlooked the publishers will be pleased to make the necessary arrangements at the first opportunity.

H/W
• Anderson Shelter
• page 107
• worksheet
• project: Nuclear age